PENGUIN 

PENGUIN SELECTED

GENERAL EDITOR: CH

WILLIAM BARNES: SELECTED POEMS

WILLIAM BARNES (1801–86) was born near Sturminster Newtown in Dorset of a farming family. He learned Greek, Latin and music, taught himself wood-engraving, and in 1823 became a schoolmaster in Mere. He married in 1827 and in 1835 moved to Dorchester. He was deeply interested in grammar and language, studied French, Italian, Welsh, Hebrew, Hindustani and other languages, and waged a lifelong campaign to rid English of classical and foreign influences. In 1837 he began studying for a Bachelor's degree of Divinity at St John's, Cambridge, and was ordained in 1848. He took up the living of Whitcombe, moving to Winterborne Came in 1862, when he gave up teaching. Among his best-known books of poetry are *Poems of Rural Life in the Dorset Dialect* (1844), *Hwomely Rhymes* (1859), both of which are written in the Dorset dialect, and *Poems of Rural Life in Common English* (1868). He was greatly interested in the techniques of verse, and the wide variety of his forms especially intrigued Thomas Hardy. Other admirers of his poetry included Tennyson, Gerard Manley Hopkins and Edmund Gosse. His work has often been praised for its evocation of the Dorset landscape, country customs and childhood scenes. As this edition makes clear, he also wrote political poems of great power and diversity, and was a master elegist.

ANDREW MOTION was born in 1952. His collections of poems include *Dangerous Play* (1985), *Love in a Life* (1991) and *The Price of Everything* (1994). He has also written critical studies of Edward Thomas and Philip Larkin, and biographies of the Lambert family and of Philip Larkin. His work has been awarded the John Llewellyn Rhys Memorial Prize, the Arvon/*Observer* Poetry Prize, the Dylan Thomas Award, the Somerset Maugham Award, and – in 1993 – the Whitbread Prize for Biography.

William Barnes

Selected Poems

EDITED WITH NOTES BY
ANDREW MOTION

PENGUIN BOOKS

PENGUIN BOOKS

Published by the Penguin Group
Penguin Books Ltd, 27 Wrights Lane, London W8 5TZ, England
Penguin Books USA Inc., 375 Hudson Street, New York, New York 10014, USA
Penguin Books Australia Ltd, Ringwood, Victoria, Australia
Penguin Books Canada Ltd, 10 Alcorn Avenue, Toronto, Ontario, Canada M4V 3B2
Penguin Books (NZ) Ltd, 182–190 Wairau Road, Auckland 10, New Zealand

Penguin Books Ltd, Registered Offices: Harmondsworth, Middlesex, England

This selection first published in Penguin Books 1994
10 9 8 7 6 5 4 3 2 1

Set in 10/11½ pt Monophoto Ehrhardt by
Datix International Limited, Bungay, Suffolk
Printed in England by Clays Ltd, St Ives plc

Contents

Acknowledgements

I am indebted to the staff of the Dorset County Museum and the British Library for the help they gave me while I worked on this book.

I am also grateful to Alan Chedzoy, Trevor Hearl, Ted Langford, Christopher Ricks – and, as always, my wife, Jan Dalley.

Note on the Text and Punctuation

For my selection of dialect poetry written by William Barnes and published during his lifetime, I have used his *Poems of Rural Life in the Dorset Dialect*, 1879 – which incorporates his dialect volumes published in 1844, 1859 and 1862, and was the last text he revised himself. In this copy-text I have silently corrected a number of small typographical errors.

For the text of dialect poems not published by Barnes during his lifetime, I have used manuscripts in the Dorset County Museum: details appear in my notes.

My selection of Barnes's poems written in standard English is drawn from his *Poems Partly of Rural Life in National English*, 1846 and *Poems of Rural Life in Common English*, 1868 – and incorporates his subsequent revisions of these volumes – and also from a handful of other sources. Once again, details appear in my notes.

Throughout the dialect poems, I have restored the grave accents that are omitted in all recent editions of Barnes's poems; readers will find these accents helpful as pointers to rhythm and pronunciation.

Some Notes on Dorset Word-shapes

1. In *Poems of Rural Life in the Dorset Dialect*, 1879 Barnes gave 'a few hints on Dorset word-shapes'. The main sounds are:

i	*ee* in beet	v	*a* in father
ii	*e* in Dorset (a sound between (i) and (iii))	vi	*aw* in awe
iii	*a* in mate	vii	*o* in dote
iv	*i* in birth	viii	*oo* in rood

2. Dorset speech often has two sounds where standard English has one. Barnes used diaereses in his poems to indicate this. Other commonly used Dorset sounds are:

Dorset	d	*Standard*	th
	-ing		-en
	v		f
	z		s

3. Some words of unlike meanings which are sounded alike in standard English are not sounded alike in Dorset. For instance:

Dorset	twold (vii above)	*Standard*	told
	toll'd		toll'd
	meäre (i & iii)		mare
	mayor (v & i)		mayor
	païl (v & i)		pail
	peäle (i & iii)		pale

4. Dorset speech distinguishes between two classes of things:
a) personal things (e.g. man), for which the personal pronoun is 'he' and the demonstrative pronoun 'this' or 'that';
b) impersonal things (e.g. water), for which the personal pronoun is 'it', and the demonstrative pronoun 'this' or 'that'.

The objective case of 'he' is 'en', and of 'them', 'em'.

5. In Dorset speech, perfect participles often affix 'a–'.

6. In Dorset speech there are forms of strong and weak verbs which do not – or do not any longer – appear in standard English, for instance:

Dorset		*Standard*	
	scrope		scraped
	clomb		climbed

Table of Dates

1801 William Barnes is born at Rush-Hay, Bagber Common, Dorset, the third child of John and Grace Barnes: the exact day and month of his birth are unknown. His grandfather had inherited but been forced to sell a farm of his own; his father was a tenant farmer who described himself in a Population Return compiled this year as a 'labourer in husbandry'.

1806 Mother dies. Barnes is sent to live at Pentridge in the Vale of Blackmore with his uncle and aunt, Charles and Ann Rabbetts, who have eight children of their own.

For the next eight years he attends the Church of England endowed school in Sturminster Newton. His education, his daughter Lucy wrote later, 'could have been nothing but elementary [but] this was of no importance, for the learning which made his name was *no grammar school knowledge* . . . no school teaching gave him his faculty of penetrating to the root of every study which came his way, it was the natural instinct of a keen and penetrative mind.'

1814 Charles Rabbetts goes bankrupt; Pentridge farm sold.

Barnes becomes a clerk with Thomas Dashwood, a solicitor in Dorchester.

1818 Dashwood dies, and Barnes becomes a clerk to Thomas Coombs, another solicitor in Dorchester.

1819 Barnes meets Julia Miles, born 1805, the daughter of James Miles, a supervisor of excises who this year moves from Saffron Walden in Essex to Dorchester.

1820 *Poetical Pieces.*

1822 *Orra: A Lapland Tale* (a narrative poem influenced by Ambrose Philips's *A Lapland Song*, which Barnes read in the *Spectator*).

1823 Moves, alone, to Mere in Wiltshire, a small market town (population 2,500) thirty miles north of Dorchester, to take up the post of headmaster at Market House School.

1825 The Miles family leave Dorchester and settle in Nailsea, Somerset.

1827 19 July: Marries Julia Miles.
Moves into Chantry House, Mere.
Etymological Dictionary.
Begins publishing essays in *Dorset County Chronicle*. In years to come he also writes for the *Gentleman's Magazine*, *Fraser's Magazine*, the *Reader*, and *Macmillan's Magazine*.

1830 The 'Swing' riots, protesting about working conditions of agricultural labourers, blaze through many counties in the south of England, including Dorset.

1833 Barnes returns to Dorchester, where he becomes headmaster of school in Durngate Street.

1834 Begins writing poems in Dorset dialect and publishing them in the *Dorset County Chronicle*. The earliest poems are prompted by the same unrest that inspired the 'Swing' riots.

1837 Moves school to Norman House in South Street, Dorchester.
His son John dies, aged three, and is subsequently remembered in several poems, including 'To a Child Lost', 'The Turnstile' and 'Our Little Boy'.
Barnes puts his name on the books of St John's College, Cambridge, beginning a ten-year study for a Bachelor's Degree of Divinity (BD).

1840 Death of childhood friend Edward Fuller, who is commemorated in the poem 'The Music o' the Dead'.

1842 *The Elements of English Grammar*.

1844 *Poems of Rural Life in the Dorset Dialect*, with a Dissertation and Glossary.
Visits Caroline Norton, a literary patron and admirer of his work, in London.

1845 Co-founds Dorset County Museum.
Visits France.

1846	*Poems Partly of Rural Life in National English.*
	Applies and fails to be appointed headmaster of Hardy's Grammar School, Dorchester.
1847	Spends three terms in Cambridge, as part of requirements for BD.
1848	Ordained at Salisbury and becomes curate at Whitcombe near Dorchester.
1849	*Se Gefylsta (The Helper): An Anglo-Saxon Delectus.*
1851	Visits the Great Exhibition in London.
1852	21 June: His wife Julia dies, aged 47, leaving him in sole charge of their five children. Barnes writes 'Plorata Veris Lachrymis', the first of many elegies for her.
1853	Death of his mother-in-law.
	The fortunes of his school decline.
1854	*A Philological Grammar.*
1859	*Views of Labour and Gold.*
	Hwomely Rhymes: A Second Collection of Poems in the Dorset Dialect.
1862	*Poems of Rural Life in the Dorset Dialect: Third Collection.*
	Tiw, or a View of the Roots and Stems of the English as a Teutonic Tongue.
	Closes school.
	Given Literary Pension of £30 a year by the government.
	Takes up the living of Winterborne Came outside Dorchester.
	Barnes's dialect poems are eulogized by Coventry Patmore in *Macmillan's Magazine.*
1863	*A Grammar and Glossary of the Dorset Dialect.*
	Visited by Coventry Patmore.
1864	Twice meets William Allingham.
1865	Visits Tennyson at Farringford, on the Isle of Wight.
1867	Tennyson and Allingham visit Barnes.
1868	*Poems of Rural Life in Common English.*
1869	*Early England and the Saxon-English*, in which Barnes gives the definitive statement of his views about the English language: 'English has become a more mongrel speech by the needless inbringing of words from Latin,

	Greek, and French, instead of words which might have been found in its older form, or in the speech of landfolk over all England, or might have been formed from its own roots and stems, as wanting words have been formed in German and other purer tongues.'
1875	Founds the Dorset Field Club.
1878	*An Outline of English Speech-Craft*, in which Barnes says, 'I have shapen my teaching as that of a speech of breath-sounded words, not of lettered ones', and gives examples of his coinings to replace corrupt imports – for instance, 'skysill' (horizon), 'mind-glee' (delight), 'song-mocking' (parody), 'thing-name' (noun) and 'many-wedder' (bigamist).
1879	*Poems of Rural Life in the Dorset Dialect.*
1881	*Ruth, A Short Drama.*
1883	Last visit to the Vale of Blackmore.
1886	*A Glossary of the Dorset Dialect.*
	7 October: Barnes dies. An unsigned obituary in the *Saturday Review* says: 'There is no doubt that he is the best pastoral poet we possess, the most sincere, the most genuine, the most Theocritan; and that the dialect is but a very thin veil hiding from us some of the most delicate and finished verse written in our time.'
	11 October: Barnes's funeral, after which his friend and neighbour, Thomas Hardy, writes his elegy 'The Last Signal'.

Further Reading

POEMS

The Poems of William Barnes, ed. Bernard Jones (Centaur Press, London, and Southern Illinois University Press, 1962), 2 vols.

Select Poems of William Barnes, ed. Thomas Hardy (Henry Froude, London, 1908).

Selected Poems of William Barnes, ed. Geoffrey Grigson (Routledge & Kegan Paul, London, 1950).

William Barnes: Selected Poems, ed. Robert Nye (Carcanet, Manchester, 1972).

William Barnes the Dorset Poet, Chris Wrigley (The Dovecot Press, Stanbridge, Wimbourne, Dorset, 1984).

BIOGRAPHICAL

Lucy Baxter (Barnes's daughter, writing under the pseudonym 'Leader Scott'), *The Life of William Barnes, Poet and Philologist* (Macmillan, London, 1887).

Alan Chedzoy, *William Barnes: The Life of the Dorset Poet* (The Dovecot Press, Dorset, 1985).

Giles Dugdale, *William Barnes of Dorset* (Cassell, London, 1953).

Thomas Hardy, 'The Reverend William Barnes BD', The *Atheneum*, 16 October 1886, reprinted in *Thomas Hardy's Personal Writings*, ed. Harold Orel (Macmillan, London, 1967).

Trevor Hearl, *William Barnes the Schoolmaster* (Longmans, Dorchester, 1966).

William Turner Levy, *William Barnes: The Man and his Poems* (Longmans, Dorchester, 1960).

Charlotte H. Lindgren, *The Love Poems and Letters of William Barnes and Julia Miles* (The Dorset Record Society, 1986).

CRITICISM

E. M. Forster, 'William Barnes' (1939), *Two Cheers for Democracy* (Penguin, Harmondsworth, 1965).

Thomas Hardy, 'Poems of Rural Life in the Dorset Dialect', unsigned review in the *New Quarterly Magazine*, October 1879, reprinted in Orel. (See above. See also Introduction to *Select Poems of William Barnes*, above.)

Charlotte H. Lindgren and Laurence Keen, *William Barnes: The Dorset Engravings* (Dorset Natural History and Archaeological Society, Dorchester, 1986).

Laurence Keen, *William Barnes: The Somerset Engravings* (Somerset County Council Library Service, 1989).

Philip Larkin, 'The Poetry of William Barnes' (1962), *Required Writing* (Faber, London, 1983).

From Poems of Rural Life in the Dorset Dialect, *1879*

First Collection

(Originally *Poems of Rural Life in the Dorset Dialect*, 1844)

SPRING

The Blackbird

Ov all the birds upon the wing
Between the zunny show'rs o' spring, –
Vor all the lark, a-swingèn high,
Mid zing below a cloudless sky,
An' sparrows, clust'rèn roun' the bough,
Mid chatter to the men at plough, –
The blackbird, whisslèn in among
The boughs, do zing the gaÿest zong.

Vor we do hear the blackbird zing
10 His sweetest ditties in the spring,
When nippèn win's noo mwore do blow
Vrom northern skies, wi' sleet or snow,
But drēve light doust along between
The leäne-zide hedges, thick an' green;
An' zoo the blackbird in among
The boughs do zing the gaÿest zong.

'Tis blithe, wi' newly-open'd eyes,
To zee the mornèn's ruddy skies;
Or, out a-haulèn frith or lops
20 Vrom new-plēsh'd hedge or new vell'd copse,
To rest at noon in primrwose beds
Below the white-bark'd woak trees' heads;
But there's noo time, the whole daÿ long,
Lik' evenèn wi' the blackbird's zong.

Vor when my work is all a-done
Avore the zettèn o' the zun,
Then blushèn Jeäne do walk along
The hedge to meet me in the drong,
An' staÿ till all is dim an' dark
30 Bezides the ashen tree's white bark;
An' all bezides the blackbird's shrill
An 'runnèn evenèn-whissle's still.

An' there in bwoyhood I did rove
Wi' pryèn eyes along the drove
To vind the nest the blackbird meäde
O' grass-stalks in the high bough's sheäde:
Or clim' aloft, wi' clingèn knees,
Vor crows' aggs up in swaÿèn trees,
While frighten'd blackbirds down below
40 Did chatter o' their little foe.
An' zoo there's noo pleäce lik' the drong,
Where I do hear the blackbird's zong.

Vellèn o' the Tree

Aye, the girt elem tree out in little hwome groun'
Wer a-stannèn this mornèn, an' now's a-cut down.
Aye, the girt elem tree, so big roun' an' so high,
Where the mowers did goo to their drink, an' did lie
In the sheäde ov his head, when the zun at his heighth
Had a-drove em vrom mowèn, wi' het an' wi' drith,
Where the haÿ-meäkers put all their picks an' their reäkes,
An' did squot down to snabble their cheese an' their
ceäkes,
An' did vill vrom their flaggons their cups wi' their eäle,
10 An' did meäke theirzelves merry wi' joke an wi' teäle.

Ees, we took up a rwope an' we tied en all round
At the top o'n, wi' woone end a-hangèn to ground,
An' we cut, near the ground, his girt stem a'most drough,
An' we bent the wold head o'n wi' woone tug or two;
An' he swaÿ'd all his limbs, an' he nodded his head,
Till he vell away down like a pillar o' lead:
An' as we did run vrom en, there, clwose at our backs,
Oh! his boughs come to groun' wi' sich whizzes an' cracks;
An' his top wer so lofty that, now he is down,
20 The stem o'n do reach a'most over the groun'.
Zoo the girt elem tree out in little hwome groun',
Wer a-stannèn this mornèn, an' now's a-cut down.

Evenèn in the Village

Now the light o' the west is a-turn'd to gloom,
An' the men be at hwome vrom ground;
An' the bells be a-zendèn all down the Coombe
From tower, their mwoansome sound.
An' the wind is still,
An' the house-dogs do bark,
An' the rooks be a-vled to the elems high an' dark,
An' the water do roar at mill.

An' the flickerèn light drough the window-peäne
10 Vrom the candle's dull fleäme do shoot,
An' young Jemmy the smith is a-gone down leäne,
A-plaÿèn his shrill-vaïced flute.
An' the miller's man
Do zit down at his ease
On the seat that is under the cluster o' trees,
Wi' his pipe an' his cider can.

Maÿ

Come out o' door, 'tis Spring! 'tis Maÿ!
The trees be green, the vields be gaÿ;
The weather's warm, the winter blast,
Wi' all his traïn o' clouds, is past;
The zun do rise while vo'k do sleep,
To teäke a higher daily zweep,
Wi' cloudless feäce a-flingèn down
His sparklèn light upon the groun'.

The aïr's a-streamèn soft, – come drow
10 The windor open; let it blow
In drough the house, where vire, an' door
A-shut, kept out the cwold avore.
Come, let the vew dull embers die,
An' come below the open sky;
An' wear your best, vor fear the groun'
In colours gaÿ mid sheäme your gown:
An' goo an' rig wi' me a mile
Or two up over geäte an' stile,
Drough zunny parrocks that do leäd,
20 Wi' crooked hedges, to the meäd,
Where elems high, in steätely ranks,
Do rise vrom yollow cowslip-banks,
An' birds do twitter vrom the spraÿ
O' bushes deck'd wi' snow-white maÿ;
An' gil'cups, wi' the deäisy bed,
Be under ev'ry step you tread.

We'll wind up roun' the hill, an' look
All down the thickly-timber'd nook,
Out where the squier's house do show
30 His grey-wall'd peaks up drough the row
O' sheädy elems, where the rook
Do build her nest; an' where the brook

Do creep along the meäds, an' lie
To catch the brightness o' the sky;
An' cows, in water to theïr knees,
Do stan' a-whiskèn off the vlees.

Mother o' blossoms, and ov all
That's feäir a-vield vrom Spring till Fall,
The gookoo over white-weäv'd seas
40 Do come to zing in thy green trees,
An' buttervlees, in giddy flight,
Do gleäm the mwost by thy gaÿ light.
Oh! when, at last, my fleshly eyes
Shall shut upon the vields an' skies,
Mid zummer's zunny days be gone,
An' winter's clouds be comèn on:
Nor mid I draw upon the e'th,
O' thy sweet aïr my leätest breath;
Alassen I mid want to staÿ
50 Behine' for thee, O flow'ry Maÿ!

Eclogue: The 'Lotments

JOHN AND RICHARD

JOHN
Zoo you be in your groun' then, I do zee,
A-workèn and a-zingèn lik' a bee.
How do it answer? what d'ye think about it?
D'ye think 'tis better wi' it than without it?
A-reck'nèn rent, an' time, an' zeed to stock it,
D'ye think that you be any thing in pocket?

RICHARD
O, 'tis a goodish help to woone, I'm sure o't.
If I had not a-got it, my poor bwones
Would now ha' eäch'd a-crackèn stwones
10 Upon the road; I wish I had zome mwore o't.

JOHN
I wish the girt woones had a-got the greäce
To let out land lik this in ouer pleäce;
But I do fear there'll never be nwone vor us,
An I can't tell whatever we shall do:
We be a most a-starvèn, an' we'd goo
To 'merica, if we'd enough to car us.

RICHARD
Why 'twer the squire, good now! a worthy man,
That vu'st brought into ouer pleäce the plan;
He zaid he'd let a vew odd eäcres
20 O' land to us poor leäb'rèn men;
An', faïth, he had enough o' teäkers
Vor that, an' twice so much ageän.
Zoo I took zome here, near my hovel,
To exercise my speäde an' shovel;
An' what wi' dungèn, diggèn up, an' zeedèn,
A-thinnèn, cleänèn, howèn up an' weedèn,
I, an' the biggest o' the childern too,
Do always vind some useful jobs to do.

JOHN
Aye, wi' a bit o' ground, if woone got any,
30 Woone's bwoys can soon get out an' eärn a penny;
An' then, by workèn, they do learn the vaster
The way to do things when they have a meäster;
Vor woone must know a deäl about the land
Bevore woone's fit to lend a useful hand,
In geärden or a-vield upon a farm.

RICHARD
An' then the work do keep em out o' harm;
Vor vo'ks that don't do nothèn wull be vound
Soon doèn woorse than nothèn, I'll be bound.
But as vor me, d'ye zee, wi' theäse here bit
40 O' land, why I have ev'ry thing a'mwost:
Vor I can fatten vowels vor the spit,
Or zell a good fat goose or two to rwoast;

An' have my beäns or cabbage, greens or grass,
Or bit o' wheat, or, sich my happy feäte is,
That I can keep a little cow, or ass,
An' a vew pigs to eat the little teäties.

JOHN
An' when your pig's a-fatted pretty well
Wi' teäties, or wi' barley an' some bran,
Why you've a-got zome vlitches vor to zell,
50 Or hang in chimney-corner, if you can.

RICHARD
Aye, that's the thing; an' when the pig do die,
We got a lot ov offal vor to fry,
An' netlèns vor to bwoil; or put the blood in,
An' meäke a meal or two o' good black-pudden.

JOHN
I'd keep myzelf from parish, I'd be bound,
If I could get a little patch o' ground.

SUMMER

Uncle an' Aunt

How happy uncle us'd to be
O' zummer time, when aunt an' he
O' Zunday evenèns, eärm in eärm,
Did walk about their tiny farm,
While birds did zing an' gnats did zwarm,
Drough grass a'most above their knees,
An' roun' by hedges an' by trees
   Wi' leafy boughs a-swaÿen.

His hat wer broad, his cwoat wer brown,
10 Wi' two long flaps a-hangèn down;
An' vrom his knee went down a blue
Knit stockèn to his buckled shoe;
An' aunt did pull her gown-taïl drough
Her pocket-hole, to keep en neat,
As she mid walk, or teäke a seat
   By leafy boughs a-swaÿèn.

An' vu'st they'd goo to zee their lots
O' pot-eärbs in the geärden plots;
An' he, i'-may-be, by the hatch,
20 Would zee aunt's vowls upon a patch
O' zeeds, an' vow if he could catch
Em wi' his gun, they shoudden vlee
Noo mwore into their roostèn tree
   Wi' leafy boughs a-swaÿèn.

An' then vrom geärden they did pass
Drough orcha'd out to zee the grass,
An' if the apple-blooth, so white,
Mid be at all a-touch'd wi' blight;
An' uncle, happy at the zight,
30 Did guess what cider there mid be
In all the orcha'd, tree wi' tree
   Wi' tutties all a-swaÿèn.

An' then they stump'd along vrom there
A-vield, to zee the cows an' meäre;
An' she, when uncle come in zight,
Look'd up, an' prick'd her ears upright,
An' whicker'd out wi' all her might;
An' he, a-chucklèn, went to zee
The cows below the sheädy tree
40 Wi' leafy boughs a-swaÿèn.

An' last ov all, they went to know
How vast the grass in meäd did grow;
An' then aunt zaid 'twer time to goo
In hwome, – a-holdèn up her shoe,
To show how wet he wer wi' dew.
An' zoo they toddled hwome to rest,
Lik' doves a-vleèn to their nest
In leafy boughs a-swaÿèn.

Hay-Meäkèn

'Tis merry ov a zummer's day,
Where vo'k be out a-meäkèn haÿ;
Where men an' women, in a string,
Do ted or turn the grass, an' zing,
Wi' cheemèn vaïces, merry zongs,
A-tossèn o' their sheenèn prongs
Wi' eärms a-zwangèn left an' right,
In colour'd gowns an' shirtsleeves white;
Or, wider spread, a-reäkèn round
10 The rwosy hedges o' the ground,
Where Sam do zee the speckled sneäke,
An' try to kill en wi' his reäke;
An Poll do jump about an' squall,
To zee the twistèn slooworm crawl.

'Tis merry where a gaÿ-tongued lot
Ov haÿ-meäkers be all a-squot,

On lightly-russlèn haÿ, a-spread
Below an elem's lofty head,
To rest their weary limbs an' munch
20 Their bit o' dinner, or their nunch;
Where teethy reäkes do lie all round
By picks a-stuck up into ground.
An' wi' their vittles in their laps,
An' in their hornen cups their draps
O' cider sweet, or frothy eäle,
Their tongues do run wi' joke an' teäle.

An' when the zun, so low an' red,
Do sheen above the leafy head
O' zome broad tree, a-rizèn high
30 Avore the vi'ry western sky,
'Tis merry where all han's do goo
Athirt the groun', by two an' two,
A-reäkèn, over humps an' hollors,
The russlèn grass up into rollers.
An' woone do row it into line,
An' woone do clwose it up behine;
An' after them the little bwoys
Do stride an' fling their eärms all woys,
Wi' busy picks, an' proud young looks
40 A-meäkèn up their tiny pooks.
An' zoo 'tis merry out among
The vo'k in haÿ-vield all day long.

The Clote

(WATER-LILY)

O zummer clote! when the brook's a-glidèn
So slow an' smooth down his zedgy bed,
Upon thy broad leaves so seäfe a-ridèn
The water's top wi' thy yollow head,

By alder's heads, O,
An' bulrush beds, O,
Thou then dost float, goolden zummer clote!

The grey-bough'd withy's a-leänèn lowly
Above the water thy leaves do hide;
10 The bendèn bulrush, a-swaÿèn slowly,
Do skirt in zummer thy river's zide;
An' perch in shoals, O,
Do vill the holes, O,
Where thou dost float, goolden zummer clote!

Oh! when thy brook-drinkèn flow'r 's a-blowèn,
The burnèn zummer's a-zettèn in;
The time o' greenness, the time o' mowèn,
When in the haÿ-vield, wi' zunburnt skin,
The vo'k do drink, O,
20 Upon the brink, O,
Where thou dost float, goolden zummer clote!

Wi' eärms a-spreadèn, an' cheäks a-blowèn,
How proud wer I when I vu'st could zwim
Athirt the pleäce where thou bist a-growèn,
Wi' thy long more vrom the bottom dim;
While cows, knee-high, O,
In brook, wer nigh, O,
Where thou dost float, goolden zummer clote!

Ov all the brooks drough the meäds a-windèn,
30 Ov all the meäds by a river's brim,
There's nwone so feäir o' my own heart's vindèn,
As where the maïdens do zee thee zwim,
An' stan' to teäke, O,
Wi' long-stemm'd reäke, O,
Thy flow'r afloat, goolden zummer clote!

Polly be-èn Upzides wi' Tom

Ah! yesterday, d'ye know, I voun'
Tom Dumpy's cwoat an' smock-frock, down
Below the pollard out in groun';
An' zoo I slyly stole
An' took the smock-frock up, an' tack'd
The sleeves an' collar up, an' pack'd
Zome nice sharp stwones, all fresh a-crack'd,
'Ithin each pocket-hole.

An' in the evenèn, when he shut
10 Off work, an' come an' donn'd his cwoat,
Their edges gi'ed en sich a cut,
How we did stan' an' laugh!
An' when the smock-frock I'd a-zow'd
Kept back his head an' hands, he drow'd
Hizzelf about, an' teäv'd, an' blow'd,
Lik' any up-tied calf.

Then in a veag away he flung
His frock, an' after me he sprung,
An' mutter'd out sich dreats, an' wrung
20 His vist up sich a size!
But I, a-runnèn, turn'd an' drow'd
Some doust, a-pick'd up vrom the road,
Back at en wi' the wind, that blow'd
It right into his eyes.

An' he did blink, an' vow he'd catch
Me zomehow yet, an' be my match.
But I wer nearly down to hatch
Avore he got vur on;
An' up in chammer, nearly dead
30 Wi' runnèn, lik' a cat I vled,
An' out o' window put my head
To zee if he wer gone.

An' there he wer, a-prowlèn roun'
Upon the green; an' I look'd down
An' told en that I hoped he voun'
He mussen think to peck
Upon a body zoo, nor whip
The meäre to drow me off, nor tip
Me out o' cart ageän, nor slip
40 Cut hoss-heäir down my neck.

Be'mi'ster

Sweet Be'mi'ster, that bist a-bound
By green an' woody hills all round,
Wi' hedges reachèn up between
A thousan' vields o' zummer green,
Where elems' lofty heads do drow
Their sheädes vor haÿ-meäkers below,
An' wild hedge-flow'rs do charm the souls
O' maïdens in their evenèn strolls.

When I o' Zunday nights wi' Jeäne
10 Do saunter drough a vield or leäne,
Where elder-blossoms be a-spread
Above the eltrot's milk-white head,
An' flow'rs o' blackberries do blow
Upon the brembles, white as snow,
To be outdone avore my zight
By Jeäne's gaÿ frock o' dazzlèn white;

Oh! then there's nothèn that's 'ithout
Thy hills that I do ho about, –
Noo bigger pleäce, noo gaÿer town,
20 Beyond thy sweet bells' dyèn soun',
As they do ring, or strike the hour,
At evenèn vrom thy wold red tow'r.
No: shelter still my head, an' keep
My bwones when I do vall asleep.

FALL

Out a-Nuttèn

Last week, when we'd a-haul'd the crops,
We went a-nuttèn out in copse,
Wi' nuttèn-bags to bring hwome vull,
An' beaky nuttèn-crooks to pull
The bushes down; an' all o's wore
Wold clothes that wer in rags avore,
An' look'd, as we did skip an' zing,
Lik' merry gipsies in a string,
A-gwaïn a-nuttèn.

10 Zoo drough the stubble, over rudge
An' vurrow, we begun to trudge;
An' Sal an' Nan agreed to pick
Along wi' me, an' Poll wi' Dick;
An' they went where the wold wood, high
An' thick, did meet an' hide the sky;
But we thought we mid vind zome good
Ripe nuts among the shorter wood,
The best vor nuttèn.

We voun' zome bushes that did feäce
20 The downcast zunlight's highest pleäce,
Where clusters hung so ripe an' brown,
That some slipp'd shell an' vell to groun'.
But Sal wi' me zoo hitch'd her lag
In brembles, that she coulden wag;
While Poll kept clwose to Dick, an' stole
The nuts vrom's hinder pocket-hole,
While he did nutty.

An' Nanny thought she zaw a sneäke,
An' jump'd off into zome girt breäke,
30 An' tore the bag where she'd a-put
Her sheäre, an' shatter'd ev'ry nut.

An' out in vield we all zot roun'
A white-stemm'd woak upon the groun',
Where yollor evenèn light did strik'
Drough yollow leaves, that still wer thick
In time o' nuttèn,

An' twold ov all the luck we had
Among the bushes, good an' bad!
Till all the maïdens left the bwoys,
40 An' skipp'd about the leäze all woys
Vor musherooms, to car back zome,
A treat vor father in at hwome.
Zoo off we trudg'd wi' clothes in slents
An' libbets, jis' lik' Jack-o'-lents,
Vrom copse a-nuttèn.

Meäple Leaves be Yollow

Come, let's stroll down so vur's the poun',
Avore the sparklèn zun is down:
The zummer's gone, an' days so feäir
As theäse be now a-gettèn reäre.
The night, wi' mwore than daylight's sheäre
O' wat'ry sky, do wet wi' dew
The eegrass up above woone's shoe,
An' meäple leaves be yollow.

The last hot doust, above the road,
10 An' vu'st dead leaves ha' been a-blow'd
By plaÿsome win's where spring did spread
The blossoms that the zummer shed;
An' near blue sloos an' conkers red
The evenèn zun, a-zettèn soon,
Do leäve a-quiv'rèn to the moon,
The meäple leaves so yollow.

Zoo come along, an' let's injaÿ
The last fine weather while do staÿ;
While thou canst hang, wi' ribbons slack,
20 Thy bonnet down upon thy back,
Avore the winter, cwold an' black,
Do kill thy flowers, an' avore
Thy bird-cage is a-took in door,
Though meäple leaves be yollow.

Shrodon Feäir

THE VU'ST PEÄRT

An' zoo's the day wer warm an' bright,
An' nar a cloud wer up in zight,
We wheedled father vor the meäre
An' cart, to goo to Shrodon feäir.
An' Poll an' Nan run off up stairs,
To shift their things, as wild as heäres;
An' pull'd out, each o'm vrom her box,
Their snow-white leäce an' newest frocks,
An' put their bonnets on, a-lined
10 Wi' blue, an' sashes tied behind;
An' turn'd avore the glass their feäce
An' back, to zee their things in pleäce;
While Dick an' I did brush our hats
An' cwoats, an' cleän ourzelves lik' cats.
At woone or two o'clock, we vound
Ourzelves at Shrodon seäfe and sound,
A-struttèn in among the rows
O' tilted stannèns an' o' shows,
An' girt long booths wi' little bars
20 Chock-vull o' barrels, mugs, an' jars,
An' meat a-cookèn out avore
The vier at the upper door;
Where zellers bwold to buyers shy
Did hollow round us, 'What d'ye buy?'

An' scores o' merry tongues did speak
At woonce, an childern's pipes did squeak,
An' horns did blow, an' drums did rumble,
An' bawlèn merrymen did tumble;
An' woone did all but want an edge
30 To peärt the crowd wi', lik' a wedge.

We zaw the dancers in a show
Dance up an' down, an' to an' fro,
Upon a rwope, wi' chalky zoles,
So light as magpies up on poles;
An' tumblers, wi' their streaks an' spots,
That all but tied theirzelves in knots.
An' then a conjurer burn'd off
Poll's han'kerchief so black's a snoff,
An' het en, wi' a single blow,
40 Right back ageän so white as snow.
An' after that, he fried a fat
Girt ceäke inzide o' my new hat;
An' yet, vor all he did en brown,
He didden even zweal the crown.

Shrodon Feäir

THE REST O'T

An' after that we met wi' zome
O' Mans'on vo'k, but jist a-come,
An' had a raffle vor a treat
All roun', o' gingerbread to eat;
An' Tom meäde leäst, wi' all his sheäkes,
An' païd the money vor the ceäkes,
But wer so lwoth to put it down
As if a penny wer a poun'.
Then up come zidelèn Sammy Heäre,
10 That's fond o' Poll, an' she can't bear,
A-holdèn out his girt scram vist,
An' ax'd her, wi' a grin an' twist,

To have zome nuts; an' she, to hide
Her laughèn, turn'd her head azide,
An' answer'd that she'd rather not,
But Nancy mid. An' Nan, so hot
As vier, zaid 'twer quite enough
Vor Poll to answer vor herzuf:
She had a tongue, she zaid, an' wit
20 Enough to use en, when 'twer fit.
An' in the dusk, a-ridèn round
Drough Okford, who d'ye think we vound
But Sam ageän, a-gwaïn vrom feäir
Astride his broken-winded meäre.
An' zoo, a-hettèn her, he tried
To keep up clwose by ouer zide:
But when we come to Haÿward-brudge,
Our Poll gi'ed Dick a meänèn nudge,
An' wi' a little twitch our meäre
30 Flung out her lags so light's a heäre,
An' left poor Sammy's skin an' bwones
Behind, a-kickèn o' the stwones.

Eclogue: The Common a-Took in

THOMAS AN' JOHN

THOMAS
Good morn t'ye, John. How b'ye? how b'ye?
Zoo you be gwaïn to market, I do zee.
Why, you be quite a-lwoaded wi' your geese.

JOHN
Ees, Thomas, ees.
Why, I'm a-gettèn rid ov ev'ry goose
An' goslèn I've a-got: an' what is woose,
I fear that I must zell my little cow.

THOMAS
How zoo, then, John? Why, what's the matter now?

What, can't ye get along? B'ye run a-ground?
10 An' can't paÿ twenty shillèns vor a pound?
What, can't ye put a lwoaf on shelf?

JOHN

Ees, now;
But I do fear I shan't 'ithout my cow.
No; they do meän to teäke the moor in, I do hear,
An' 'twill be soon begun upon;
Zoo I must zell my bit o' stock to-year,
Because they woon't have any groun' to run upon.

THOMAS

Why, what d'ye tell o'? I be very zorry
To hear what they be gwaïn about;
But yet I s'pose there'll be a 'lotment vor ye,
20 When they do come to mark it out.

JOHN

No; not vor me, I fear. An' if there should,
Why 'twoulden be so handy as 'tis now;
Vor 'tis the common that do do me good,
The run vor my vew geese, or vor my cow.

THOMAS

Ees, that's the job; why 'tis a handy thing
To have a bit o' common, I do know,
To put a little cow upon in Spring,
The while woone's bit ov orcha'd grass do grow.

JOHN

Aye, that's the thing, you zee. Now I do mow
30 My bit o' grass, an' meäke a little rick;
An' in the zummer, while do grow,
My cow do run in common vor to pick
A bleäde or two o' grass, if she can vind em,
Vor tother cattle don't leäve much behind em.
Zoo in the evenèn, we do put a lock
O' nice fresh grass avore the wicket;
An' she do come at vive or zix o'clock,
As constant as the zun, to pick it.

An' then, bezides the cow, why we do let
40 Our geese run out among the emmet hills;
An' then when we do pluck em, we do get
Vor zeäle zome veathers an' zome quills;
An' in the winter we do fat em well,
An' car em to the market vor to zell
To gentlevo'ks, vor we don't oft avvword
To put a goose a-top ov ouer bwoard;
But we do get our feäst, – vor we be eäble
To clap the giblets up a-top o' teäble.

THOMAS
An' I don't know o' many better things,
50 Than geese's heads and gizzards, lags an' wings.

JOHN
An' then, when I ha' nothèn else to do,
Why I can teäke my hook an' gloves, an' goo
To cut a lot o' vuzz and briars
Vor hetèn ovens, or vor lightèn viers.
An' when the children be too young to eärn
A penny, they can g'out in zunny weather,
An' run about, an' get together
A bag o' cow-dung vor to burn.

THOMAS
'Tis handy to live near a common;
60 But I've a-zeed, an' I've a-zaid,
That if a poor man got a bit o' bread,
They'll try to teäke it vrom en.
But I wer twold back tother day,
That they be got into a way
O' lettèn bits o' groun' out to the poor.

JOHN
Well, I do hope 'tis true, I'm sure;
An' I do hope that they will do it here,
Or I must goo to workhouse, I do fear.

WINTER

What Dick an' I Did

Last week the Browns ax'd nearly all
  The naïghbours to a randy,
An' left us out o't, girt an' small,
  Vor all we liv'd so handy;
An' zoo I zaid to Dick, 'We'll trudge,
  When they be in their fun, min;
An' car up zome'hat to the rudge,
  An' jis' stop up the tun, min.'

Zoo, wi' the ladder vrom the rick,
10 We stole towards the house,
An' crope in roun' behind en, lik'
  A cat upon a mouse.
Then, lookèn roun', Dick whisper'd, 'How
  Is theäse job to be done, min:
Why we do want a faggot now,
  Vor stoppèn up the tun, min.'

'Stan' still,' I answer'd; 'I'll teäke ceäre
  O' that: why dussen zee
The little grindèn stwone out there,
20 Below the apple-tree?
Put up the ladder; in a crack
  Shalt zee that I wull run, min,
An' teäke en up upon my back,
  An' soon stop up the tun, min.'

Zoo up I clomb upon the thatch,
  An' clapp'd en on; an' slided
Right down ageän, an' run drough hatch,
  Behind the hedge, an' hided.
The vier that wer clear avore,
30 Begun to spweil their fun, min;
The smoke all roll'd toward the door,
  Vor I'd a-stopp'd the tun, min.

The maïdens cough'd or stopp'd their breath,
  The men did hauk an' spet;
The wold vo'k bundled out from he'th
  Wi' eyes a-runnèn wet.
''T'ool choke us all,' the wold man cried,
  'Whatever's to be done, min?
Why zome'hat is a-vell inside
40 O' chimney drough the tun, min.'

Then out they scamper'd all, vull run,
  An' out cried Tom, 'I think
The grindèn-stwone is up on tun,
  Vor I can zee the wink.
This is some kindness that the vo'k
  At Woodley have a-done, min;
I wish I had em here, I'd poke
  Their numskulls down the tun, min.'

Then off he zet, an' come so quick
50 'S a lamplighter, an' brote
The little ladder in vrom rick,
  To clear the chimney's droat.
While I, a-chucklèn at the joke,
  A-slided down, to run, min,
To hidelock, had a-left the vo'k
  As bad as na'r a tun, min.

The Happy Days When I wer Young

In happy days when I wer young,
An' had noo ho, an' laugh'd an' zung,
The maïd wer merry by her cow,
An' men wer merry wi' the plough;
But never talk'd, at hwome or out
O' doors, o' what's a-talk'd about
By many now, – that to despise
The laws o' God an' man is wise.

Wi' daïly health, an' daïly bread,
10 An' thatch above their shelter'd head,
They velt noo fear, an' had noo spite,
To keep their eyes awake at night;
But slept in peace wi' God on high
An' man below, an' fit to die.

O grassy meäd an' woody nook,
An' waters o' the windèn brook,
That sprung below the vu'st dark sky
That raïn'd, to run till seas be dry;
An' hills a-stannèn on while all
20 The works o' man do rise an' vall;
An' trees the toddlèn child do vind
At vu'st, an' leäve at last behind;
I wish that you could now unvwold
The peace an' jaÿ o' times o' wold;
An' tell, when death do still my tongue,
O' happy days when I wer young.
Vrom where wer all this venom brought,
To kill our hope an' taïnt our thought?
Clear brook! thy water coulden bring
30 Such venom vrom thy rocky spring;
Nor could it come in zummer blights,
Or reävèn storms o' winter nights,
Or in the cloud an' viry stroke
O' thunder that do split the woak.

O valley dear! I wish that I
'D a-liv'd in former times, to die
Wi' all the happy souls that trod
Thy turf in peäce, an' died to God;
Or gone wi' them that laugh'd an' zung
40 In happy days when I wer young!

In the Stillness o' the Night

Ov all the housen o' the pleäce,
There's woone where I do like to call
By day or night the best ov all,
To zee my Fanny's smilèn feäce;
An' there the steätely trees do grow,
A-rockèn as the win' do blow,
While she do sweetly sleep below,
In the stillness o' the night.

An' there, at evenèn, I do goo
10 A-hoppèn over geätes an' bars,
By twinklèn light o' winter stars,
When snow do clumper to my shoe;
An' zometimes we do slyly catch
A chat an hour upon the stratch,
An' peärt wi' whispers at the hatch
In the stillness o' the night.

An' zometimes she do goo to zome
Young naïghbours' housen down the pleäce,
An' I do get a clue to treäce
20 Her out, an' goo to zee her hwome;
An' I do wish a vield a mile,
As she do sweetly chat an' smile
Along the drove, or at the stile,
In the stillness o' the night.

The Carter

O, I be a carter, wi' my whip
A-smackèn loud, as by my zide,
Up over hill, an' down the dip,
The heavy lwoad do slowly ride.

An' I do haul in all the crops,
An' I do bring in vuzz vrom down;
An' I do goo vor wood to copse,
An' car the corn an' straw to town.

An' I do goo vor lime, an' bring
10 Hwome cider wi' my sleek-heäir'd team,
An' smack my limber whip an' zing,
While all their bells do gaïly cheeme.

An' I do always know the pleäce
To gi'e the hosses breath, or drug;
An' ev'ry hoss do know my feäce,
An' mind my *'mether ho!* an' *whug!*

An' merry haÿ-meäkers do ride
Vrom vield in zummer wi' their prongs,
In my blue waggon, zide by zide
20 Upon the reäves, a-zingèn zongs.

An' when the vrost do catch the stream,
An' oves wi' icicles be hung,
My pantèn hosses' breath do steam
In white-grass'd vields, a-haulèn dung.

An' mine's the waggon fit vor lwoads,
An' mine be lwoads to cut a rout;
An' mine's a team, in routy rwoads,
To pull a lwoaded waggon out.

A zull is nothèn when do come
30 Behind their lags; an' they do teäke
A roller as they would a drum,
An' harrow as they would a reäke.

O! I be a carter, wi' my whip
A-smackèn loud, as by my zide,
Up over hill, an' down the dip,
The heavy lwoad do slowly ride.

Eclogue: Father Come Hwome

JOHN, WIFE, AN' CHILD

CHILD
O mother, mother! be the teäties done?
Here's father now a-comèn down the track.
He's got his nitch o' wood upon his back,
An' such a speäker in en! I'll be bound,
He's long enough to reach vrom ground
Up to the top ov ouer tun;
'Tis jist the very thing vor Jack an' I
To goo a-colepecksèn wi', by an' by.

WIFE
The teäties must be ready pretty nigh;
10 Do teäke woone up upon the fork an' try.
The ceäke upon the vier, too, 's a-burnèn,
I be afeärd: do run an' zee, an' turn en.

JOHN
Well, mother! here I be woonce mwore, at hwome.

WIFE
Ah! I be very glad you be a-come.
You be a-tired an' cwold enough, I s'pose;
Zit down an' rest your bwones, an' warm your nose.

JOHN
Why I be nippy: what is there to eat?

WIFE
Your supper's nearly ready. I've a-got
Some teäties here a-doèn in the pot;
20 I wish wi' all my heart I had some meat.
I got a little ceäke too, here, a-beäkèn o'n
Upon the vier. 'Tis done by this time though.
He's nice an' moist; vor when I wer a-meäkèn o'n
I stuck some bits ov apple in the dough.

CHILD
Well, father; what d'ye think? The pig got out
This mornèn; an' avore we zeed or heärd en,
He run about, an' got out into geärden,
An' routed up the groun' zoo wi' his snout!

JOHN
Now only think o' that! You must contrive
30 To keep en in, or else he'll never thrive.

CHILD
An' father, what d'ye think? I voun' to-day
The nest where thik wold hen ov our's do lay:
'Twer out in orcha'd hedge, an' had vive aggs.

WIFE
Lo'k there: how wet you got your veet an' lags!
How did ye get in such a pickle, Jahn?

JOHN
I broke my hoss, an' been a-fwo'ced to stan'
All's day in mud an' water vor to dig,
An' meäde myzelf so wetshod as a pig.

CHILD
Father, teäke off your shoes, then come, and I
40 Will bring your wold woones vor ye, nice an' dry.

WIFE
An' have ye got much hedgen mwore to do?

JOHN
Enough to last vor dree weeks mwore or zoo.

WIFE
An' when y'ave done the job you be about,
D'ye think you'll have another vound ye out?

JOHN
O ees, there'll be some mwore: vor after that,
I got a job o' trenchèn to goo at;

An' then zome trees to shroud, an' wood to vell, –
Zoo I do hope to rub on pretty well
Till zummer time; an' then I be to cut
50 The wood an' do the trenchèn by the tut.

CHILD
An' nex' week, father, I'm a-gwaïn to goo
A-pickèn stwones, d'ye know, vor Farmer True.

WIFE
An' little Jack, you know, 's a-gwaïn to eärn
A penny too, a-keepèn birds off corn.

JOHN
O brave! What wages do 'e meän to gi'e?

WIFE
She dreppence vor a day, an' twopence he.

JOHN
Well, Polly; thou must work a little spracker
When thou bist out, or else thou wu'ten pick
A dungpot lwoad o' stwones up very quick.

CHILD
60 Oh! yes I shall. But Jack do want a clacker:
An' father, wull ye teäke an' cut
A stick or two to meäke his hut?

JOHN
You wench! why you be always up a-baggèn.
I be too tired now to-night, I'm sure,
To zet a-doèn any mwore:
Zoo I shall goo up out o' the waÿ o' the waggon.

Sundry Pieces

The Hwomestead

If I had all the land my zight
  Can overlook vrom Chalwell hill,
Vrom Sherborn left to Blanvord right,
  Why I could be but happy still.
An' I be happy wi' my spot
O' freehold ground an' mossy cot,
An' shoulden get a better lot
  If I had all my will.

My orcha'd's wide, my trees be young;
10 An' they do bear such heavy crops,
Their boughs, lik' onion-rwopes a-hung,
  Be all a-trigg'd to year, wi' props.
I got some geärden groun' to dig,
A parrock, an' a cow an' pig;
I got zome cider vor to swig,
  An' eäle o' malt an' hops.

I'm landlord o' my little farm,
  I'm king 'ithin my little pleäce;
I don't break laws, an' don't do harm,
20 An' ben't a-feär'd o' noo man's feäce.
When I'm a-cover'd wi' my thatch,
Noo man do deäre to lift my latch;
Where honest han's do shut the hatch,
  There fear do leäve the pleäce.

My lofty elem trees do screen
  My brown-ruf'd house, an' here below,
My geese do strut athirt the green,
  An' hiss an' flap their wings o' snow;

As I do walk along a rank
30 Ov apple trees, or by a bank,
Or zit upon a bar or plank,
To zee how things do grow.

Uncle out o' Debt an' out o' Danger

Ees; uncle had thik small hwomestead,
The leäzes an' the bits o' meäd,
Bezides the orcha'd in his prime,
An' copse-wood vor the winter time.
His wold black meäre, that draw'd his cart,
An' he, wer seldom long apeärt;
Vor he work'd hard an' païd his woy,
An' zung so litsome as a bwoy,
As he toss'd an' work'd,
10 An' blow'd an' quirk'd,
'I'm out o' debt an' out o' danger,
An' I can feäce a friend or stranger;
I've a vist for friends, an' I'll vind a peäir
Vor the vu'st that do meddle wi' me or my meäre.'

His meäre's long vlexy vetlocks grow'd
Down roun' her hoofs so black an' brode;
Her head hung low, her taïl reach'd down
A-bobbèn nearly to the groun'.
The cwoat that uncle mwostly wore
20 Wer long behind an' straïght avore,
An' in his shoes he had girt buckles,
An' breeches button'd round his huckles;
An' he zung wi' pride,
By's wold meäre's zide,
'I'm out o' debt an' out o' danger,
An' I can feäce a friend or stranger;
I've a vist vor friends, an' I'll vind a peäir
Vor the vu'st that do meddle wi' me or my meäre.'

An' he would work, – an' lwoad, an' shoot,
30 An' spur his heaps o' dung or zoot;
Or car out haÿ, to sar his vew
Milch cows in corners dry an' lew;
Or dreve a zyve, or work a pick,
To pitch or meäke his little rick;
Or thatch en up wi' straw or zedge,
Or stop a shard, or gap, in hedge;
An' he work'd an' flung
His eärms, an' zung
'I'm out o' debt an' out o' danger,
40 An' I can feäce a friend or stranger;
I've a vist vor friends, an' I'll vind a peäir
Vor the vu'st that do meddle wi' me or my meäre.'

An' when his meäre an' he'd a-done
Their work, an' tired ev'ry bwone,
He zot avore the vire, to spend
His evenèn wi' his wife or friend;
An' wi' his lags out-stratch'd vor rest,
An' woone hand in his wes'coat breast,
While burnèn sticks did hiss an' crack,
50 An' fleämes did bleäzy up the back,
There he zung so proud
In a bakky cloud,
'I'm out o' debt an' out o' danger,
An' I can feäce a friend or stranger;
I've a vist vor friends, an' I'll vind a peäir
Vor the vu'st that do meddle wi' me or my meäre.'

From market how he used to ride,
Wi' pots a-bumpèn by his zide
Wi' things a-bought – but not vor trust,
60 Vor what he had he païd vor vu'st;
An' when he trotted up the yard,
The calves did bleäry to be sar'd,
An' pigs did scoat all drough the muck,
An' geese did hiss, an' hens did cluck;
An' he zung aloud,
So pleased an' proud,

'I'm out o' debt an' out o' danger,
An' I can feäce a friend or stranger;
I've a vist vor friends, an' I'll vind a peäir
70 Vor the vu'st that do meddle wi' me or my meäre.'

When he wer joggèn hwome woone night
Vrom market, after candle-light,
(He mid a-took a drop o' beer,
Or midden, vor he had noo fear,)
Zome ugly, long-lagg'd, herrèn-ribs,
Jump'd out an' ax'd en vor his dibs;
But he soon gi'ed en such a mawlèn,
That there he left en down a-sprawlèn,
While he jogg'd along
80 Wi' his own wold zong,
'I'm out o' debt an' out o' danger,
An' I can feäce a friend or stranger;
I've a vist vor friends, an' I'll vind a peäir
Vor the vu'st that do meddle wi' me or my meäre.'

The Wold Waggon

The girt wold waggon uncle had,
When I wer up a hardish lad,
Did stand, a-screen'd vrom het an' wet,
In zummer at the barken geäte,
Below the elems' spreädèn boughs,
A-rubb'd by all the pigs an' cows.
An' I've a-clom his head an' zides,
A-riggèn up or jumpèn down
A-playèn, or in happy rides
10 Along the leäne or drough the groun'.
An' many souls be in their greäves,
That rod' together on his reäves;
An' he, an' all the hosses too,
'V a-ben a-done vor years agoo.

Upon his head an' taïl wer pinks,
A-païnted all in tangled links;
His two long zides wer blue, – his bed
Bent slightly upward at the head;
His reäves rose upward in a bow
20 Above the slow hind-wheels below.
Vour hosses wer a-kept to pull
The girt wold waggon when 'twer vull:
The black meäre *Smiler*, strong enough
To pull a house down by herzuf,
So big, as took my widest strides
To straddle halfway down her zides;
An' champèn *Vi'let*, sprack an' light,
That foam'd an' pull'd wi' all her might:
An' *Whitevoot*, leäzy in the treäce,
30 Wi' cunnèn looks an' snow-white feäce;
Bezides a baÿ woone, short-taïl *Jack*,
That wer a treäce-hoss or a hack.

How many lwoads o' vuzz, to scald
The milk, thik waggon have a-haul'd!
An' wood vrom copse, an' poles vor raïls,
An' bavèns wi' their bushy taïls;
An' loose-ear'd barley, hangèn down
Outzide the wheels a'móst to groun',
An' lwoads o' haÿ so sweet an' dry,
40 A-builded straïght, an' long, an' high;
An' haÿ-meäkers a-zittèn roun'
The reäves, a-ridèn hwome vrom groun',
When Jim gi'ed Jenny's lips a-smackèn,
An' jealous Dicky whipp'd his back,
An' maïdens scream'd to veel the thumps
A-gi'ed by trenches an' by humps.
But he, an' all his hosses too,
'V a-ben a-done vor years agoo.

The Common a-Took in

Oh! no, Poll, no! Since they've a-took
The common in, our lew wold nook
Don't seem a-bit as used to look
  When we had runnèn room;
Girt banks do shut up ev'ry drong,
An' stratch wi' thorny backs along
Where we did use to run among
  The vuzzen an' the broom.

Ees; while the ragged colts did crop
10 The nibbled grass, I used to hop
The emmet-buts, vrom top to top,
  So proud o' my spry jumps:
Wi' thee behind or at my zide,
A-skippèn on so light an' wide
'S thy little frock would let thee stride,
  Among the vuzzy humps.

Ah while the lark up over head
Did twitter, I did search the red
Thick bunch o' broom, or yellow bed
20   O' vuzzen vor a nest;
An' thou di'st hunt about, to meet
Wi' strawberries so red an' sweet,
Or clogs, or shoes off hosses' veet,
  Or wild thyme vor thy breast;

Or when the cows did run about
A-stung, in zummer, by the stout,
Or when they plaÿ'd, or when they foüght,
  Di'st stand a-lookèn on:
An' where white geese, wi' long red bills,
30 Did veed among the emmet-hills,
There we did goo to vind their quills
  Alongzide o' the pon'.

What fun there wer among us, when
The haÿward come, wi' all his men,
To drève the common, an' to pen
  Strange cattle in the pound;
The cows did bleäre, the men did shout
An' toss their eärms an' sticks about,
An' vo'ks, to own their stock, come out
40 Vrom all the housen round.

The Väices that be Gone

When evenèn sheädes o' trees do hide
A body by the hedge's zide,
An' twitt'rèn birds, wi' plaÿsome flight,
Do vlee to roost at comèn night,
Then I do saunter out o' zight
  In orcha'd, where the pleäce woonce rung
  Wi' laughs a-laugh'd an' zongs a-zung
    By vaïces that be gone.

There's still the tree that bore our swing,
10 An' others where the birds did zing;
But long-leav'd docks do overgrow
The groun' we trampled beäre below,
Wi' merry skippèns to an' fro
  Bezide the banks, where Jim did zit
  A-plaÿèn o' the clarinit
    To vaïces that be gone.

How mother, when we us'd to stun
Her head wi' all our naïsy fun,
Did wish us all a-gone vrom hwome:
20 An' now that zome be dead, an' zome
A-gone, an' all the pleäce is dum',
  How she do wish, wi' useless tears,
  To have ageän about her ears
    The vaïces that be gone.

Vor all the maïdens an' the bwoys
But I, be marri'd off all woys,
Or dead an' gone; but I do bide
At hwome, alwone, at mother's zide,
An' often, at the evenèn-tide,
30 I still do saunter out, wi' tears,
Down drough the orcha'd, where my ears
Do miss the vaïces gone.

The Music o' the Dead

When music, in a heart that's true,
Do kindle up wold loves anew,
An' dim wet eyes, in feäirest lights,
Do zee but inward fancy's zights;
When creepèn years, wi' with'rèn blights,
'V a-took off them that wer so dear,
How touchèn 'tis if we do hear
The tuèns o' the dead, John.

When I, a-stannèn in the lew
10 O' trees a storm's a-beätèn drough,
Do zee the slantèn mist a-drove
By spitevul winds along the grove,
An' hear their hollow sounds above
My shelter'd head, do seem, as I
Do think o' zunny days gone by,
Lik' music vor the dead, John.

Last night, as I wer gwaïn along
The brook, I heärd the milk-maïd's zong
A-ringèn out so clear an' shrill
20 Along the meäds an' roun' the hill.
I catch'd the tuèn, an' stood still
To hear't; 'twer woone that Jeäne did zing
A-vield a-milkèn in the spring, –
Sweet music o' the dead, John.

Don't tell o' zongs that be a-zung
By young chaps now, wi' sheämeless tongue:
Zing me wold ditties, that would start
The maïdens' tears, or stir my heart
To teäke in life a manly peärt, –
30 The wold vo'k's zongs that twold a teäle,
An' vollow'd round their mugs o' eäle,
The music o' the dead, John.

Jeäne

We now mid hope vor better cheer,
My smilèn wife o' twice vive year.
Let others frown, if thou bist near
Wi' hope upon thy brow, Jeäne;
Vor I vu'st lov'd thee when thy light
Young sheäpe vu'st grew to woman's height;
I loved thee near, an' out o' zight,
An' I do love thee now, Jeäne.

An' we've a-trod the sheenèn bleäde
10 Ov eegrass in the zummer sheäde,
An' when the leäves begun to feäde
Wi' zummer in the weäne, Jeäne;
An' we've a-wander'd drough the groun'
O' swaÿèn wheat a-turnèn brown,
An' we've a-stroll'd together roun'
The brook an' drough the leäne, Jeäne.

An' nwone but I can ever tell
Ov all thy tears that have a-vell
When trials meäde thy bosom zwell,
20 An' nwone but thou o' mine, Jeäne;
An' now my heart, that heav'd wi' pride
Back then to have thee at my zide,
Do love thee mwore as years do slide,
An' leäve them times behine, Jeäne.

The Hwomestead a-Vell into Hand

The house where I wer born an' bred,
Did own his woaken door, John,
When vu'st he shelter'd father's head,
An' gramfer's long avore, John.
An' many a ramblèn happy chile,
An' chap so strong an' bwold,
An' bloomèn maïd wi' plaÿsome smile,
Did call their hwome o' wold
Thik ruf so warm,
10 A-kept vrom harm
By elem trees that broke the storm.

An' in the orcha'd out behind,
The apple-trees in row, John,
Did swaÿ wi' moss about their rind
Their heads a-noddèn low, John.
An' there, bezide zome groun' vor corn,
Two strips did skirt the road;
In woone the cow did toss her horn,
While tother wer a-mow'd,
20 In June, below
The lofty row
Ov trees that in the hedge did grow.

A-workèn in our little patch
O' parrock, rathe or leäte, John,
We little ho'd how vur mid stratch
The squier's wide esteäte, John.
Our hearts, so honest an' so true,
Had little vor to fear;
Vor we could paÿ up all their due,
30 An' gi'e a friend good cheer
At hwome, below
The lofty row
O' trees a-swaÿèn to an' fro.

An' there in het, an' there in wet,
  We tweil'd wi' busy hands, John;
Vor ev'ry stroke o' work we het,
  Did better our own lands, John.
But after me, ov all my kin,
  Not woone can hold em on;
40 Vor we can't get a life put in
  Vor mine, when I'm a-gone
    Vrom thik wold brown
    Thatch ruf, a-boun'
By elem trees a-growèn roun'.

Ov eight good hwomes, where I can mind
  Vo'k liv'd upon their land, John,
But dree be now a-left behind;
  The rest ha' vell in hand, John,
An' all the happy souls they ved
50 Be scatter'd vur an' wide.
An' zome o'm be a-wantèn bread,
  Zome, better off, ha' died,
    Noo mwore to ho
    Vor homes below
The trees a-swaÿèn to an' fro.

An' I could leäd ye now all round
  The parish, if I would, John,
An' show ye still the very ground
  Where vive good housen stood, John.
60 In broken orcha'ds near the spot,
  A vew wold trees do stand;
But dew do vall where vo'k woonce zot
  About the burnèn brand
    In housen warm,
    A-kept vrom harm
By elems that did break the storm.

Eclogue: The Times

JOHN AN' TOM

JOHN

Well, Tom, how be'st? Zoo thou'st a-got thy neäme
Among the leaguers, then, as I've a-heärd.

TOM

Aye, John, I have, John; an' I ben't afeärd
To own it. Why, who woulden do the seäme?
We shan't goo on lik' this long, I can tell ye.
Bread is so high an' wages be so low,
That, after workèn lik' a hoss, you know,
A man can't eärn enough to vill his belly.

JOHN

Ah! well! Now there, d'ye know, if I wer sure
10 That theäsem men would gi'e me work to do
All drough the year, an' always paÿ me mwore
Than I'm a-eärnèn now, I'd jein em too.
If I wer sure they'd bring down things so cheap,
That what mid buy a pound o' mutton now
Would buy the hinder quarters, or the sheep,
Or what wull buy a pig would buy a cow:
In short, if they could meäke a shillèn goo
In market just so vur as two,
Why then, d'ye know, I'd be their man;
20 But, hang it! I don't think they can.

TOM

Why ees they can, though you don't know't,
An' theäsem men can meäke it clear.
Why vu'st they'd zend up members ev'ry year
To Parli'ment, an' ev'ry man would vote;
Vor if a fellow midden be a squier,
He mid be just so fit to vote, an' goo
To meäke the laws at Lon'on, too,
As many that do hold their noses higher.

Why shoulden fellows meäke good laws an' speeches
30 A-dressed in fusti'n cwoats an' cord'roy breeches?
Or why should hooks an' shovels, zives an' axes,
Keep any man vrom votèn o' the taxes?
An' when the poor've a-got a sheäre
In meäkèn laws, they'll teäke good ceäre
To meäke zome good woones vor the poor.
Do stan' by reason, John; because
The men that be to meäke the laws,
Will meäke em vor theirzelves, you mid be sure.

JOHN
Ees, that they wull. The men that you mid trust
40 To help you, Tom, would help their own zelves vu'st.

TOM
Aye, aye. But we would have a better plan
O' votèn, than the woone we got. A man,
As things be now, d'ye know, can't goo an' vote
Ageän another man, but he must know't.
We'll have a box an' balls, vor votèn men
To pop their hands 'ithin, d'ye know; an' then,
If woone don't happen vor to lik' a man,
He'll drop a little black ball vrom his han',
An' zend en hwome ageän. He woon't be led
50 To choose a man to teäke away his bread.

JOHN
But if a man you midden like to 'front,
Should chance to call upon ye, Tom, zome day,
An' ax ye vor your vote, what could ye zay?
Why if you woulden answer, or should grunt
Or bark, he'd know you'd meän 'I won't.'
To promise woone a vote an' not to gi'e 't,
Is but to be a liar an' a cheät.
An' then, bezides, when he did count the balls,
An' vind white promises a-turn'd half black;
60 Why then he'd think the voters all a pack
O' rogues together, – ev'ry woone o'm false.

An' if he had the power, very soon
Perhaps he'd vall upon em, ev'ry woone.
The times be pinchèn me, so well as you,
But I can't tell what ever they can do.

TOM

Why meäke the farmers gi'e their leäbourèn men
Mwore wages, – half or twice so much ageän
As what they got.

JOHN

But, Thomas, you can't meäke
A man paÿ mwore away than he can teäke.
70 If you do meäke en gi'e, to till a vield,
So much ageän as what the groun' do yield,
He'll shut out farmèn – or he'll be a goose –
An' goo an' put his money out to use.
Wages be low because the hands be plenty;
They mid be higher if the hands wer skenty.
Leäbour, the seäme's the produce o' the vield,
Do zell at market price – jist what 't 'ill yield.
Thou wouldsten gi'e a zixpence, I do guess,
Vor zix fresh aggs, if zix did zell for less.
80 If theäsem vo'k could come an' meäke mwore lands,
If they could teäke wold England in their hands
An' stratch it out jist twice so big ageän,
They'd be a-doèn zome'hat vor us then.

TOM

But if they wer a-zent to Parli'ment
To meäke the laws, dost know, as I've a-zaid,
They'd knock the corn-laws on the head;
An' then the landlards must let down their rent,
An' we should very soon have cheaper bread:
Farmers would gi'e less money vor their lands.

JOHN

90 Aye, zoo they mid, an' prices mid be low'r
Vor what their land would yield; an' zoo their hands
Would be jist where they wer avore.

An' if theäse men wer all to hold together,
They coulden meäke new laws to change the weather!
They ben't so mighty as to think o' frightenèn
The vrost an' raïn, the thunder an' the lightenèn!
An' as vor me, I don't know what to think
O' them there fine, big-talkèn, cunnèn,
Strange men, a-comèn down vrom Lon'on.
100 Why they don't stint theirzelves, but eat an' drink
The best at public-house where they do staÿ;
They don't work gratis, they do get their paÿ.
They woulden pinch theirzelves to do us good,
Nor gi'e their money vor to buy us food.
D'ye think, if we should meet em in the street
Zome day in Lon'on, they would stand a treat?

TOM
They be a-païd, because they be a-zent
By corn-law vo'k that be the poor man's friends,
To tell us all how we mid gaïn our ends,
110 A-zendèn peäpers up to Parli'ment.

JOHN
Ah! teäke ceäre how dost trust em. Dost thou know
The funny feäble o' the pig an' crow?
Woone time a crow begun to strut an' hop
About zome groun' that men'd a-been a-drillèn
Wi' barley or zome wheat, in hopes o' villèn
Wi' good fresh corn his empty crop.
But lik' a thief, he didden like the païns
O' workèn hard to get en a vew graïns;
Zoo while the sleeky rogue wer there a-huntèn,
120 Wi' little luck, vor corns that mid be vound
A-peckèn vor, he heärd a pig a-gruntèn
Just tother zide o' hedge, in tother ground.
'Ah!' thought the cunnèn rogue, an' gi'ed a hop,
'Ah! that's the way vor me to vill my crop;
Aye, that's the plan, if nothèn don't defeät it.
If I can get thik pig to bring his snout
In here a bit an' turn the barley out,
Why, hang it! I shall only have to eat it.'

Wi' that he vled up straïght upon a woak,
130 An' bowèn, lik' a man at hustèns, spoke:
'My friend,' zaid he, 'that's poorish livèn vor ye
In thik there leäze. Why I be very zorry
To zee how they hard-hearted vo'k do sarve ye.
You can't live there. Why! do they meän to starve ye?'
'Ees,' zaid the pig, a-gruntèn, 'ees;
What wi' the hosses an' the geese,
There's only docks an' thissles here to chaw.
Instead o' livèn well on good warm straw,
I got to grub out here, where I can't pick
140 Enough to meäke me half an ounce o' flick.'
'Well,' zaid the crow, 'd'ye know, if you'll stan' that,
You mussen think, my friend, o' gettèn fat.
D'ye want some better keep? Vor if you do,
Why, as a friend, I be a-come to tell ye,
That if you'll come an' jus' get drough
Theäse gap up here, why you mid vill your belly.
Why, they've a-been a-drillèn corn, d'ye know,
In theäse here piece o' groun' below;
An' if you'll just put in your snout,
150 An' run en up along a drill,
Why, hang it! you mid grub it out,
An' eat, an' eat your vill.
There idden any feär that vo'k mid come,
Vor all the men be jist a-gone in hwome.'
The pig, believèn ev'ry single word
That wer a-twold en by the cunnèn bird
Wer only vor his good, an' that 'twer true,
Just gi'ed a grunt, an' bundled drough,
An' het his nose, wi' all his might an' maïn,
160 Right up a drill, a-routèn up the graïn;
An' as the cunnèn crow did gi'e a caw
A-praïsèn ō'n, oh! he did veel so proud!
An' work'd, an' blow'd, an' toss'd, an' plough'd
The while the cunnèn crow did vill his maw.
An' after workèn till his bwones
Did eäche, he soon begun to veel

That he should never get a meal,
Unless he dined on dirt an' stwones.
'Well,' zaid the crow, 'why don't ye eat?'
170 'Eat what, I wonder!' zaid the heäiry plougher,
A-brislèn up an' lookèn rather zour;
'I don't think dirt an' flints be any treat.'
'Well,' zaid the crow, 'why you be blind.
What! don't ye zee how thick the corn do lie
Among the dirt? An' don't ye zee how I
Do pick up all that you do leäve behind?
I'm zorry that your bill should be so snubby.'
'No,' zaid the pig, 'methinks that I do zee
My bill wull do uncommon well vor thee,
180 Vor thine wull peck, an' mine wull grubby.'
An' just wi' this a-zaid by mister Flick
To mister Crow, wold John the farmer's man
Come up, a-zwingèn in his han'
A good long knotty stick,
An' laid it on, wi' all his might,
The poor pig's vlitches, left an' right;
While mister Crow, that talk'd so fine
O' friendship, left the pig behine,
An' vled away upon a distant tree,
190 Vor pigs can only grub, but crows can vlee.

TOM
Aye, thik there teäle mid do vor children's books;
But you wull vind it hardish for ye
To frighten me, John, wi' a storry
O' silly pigs an' cunnèn rooks.
If we be grubbèn pigs, why then, I s'pose,
The farmers an' the girt woones be the crows.

JOHN
'Tis very odd there idden any friend
To poor-vo'k hereabout, but men mus' come
To do us good away from tother end
200 Ov England! Han't we any frien's near hwome?

I mus' zay, Thomas, that 'tis rather odd
That strangers should become so very civil, –
That ouer vo'k be children o' the Devil,
An' other vo'k be all the vo'k o' God!
If we've a-got a friend at all,
Why who can tell – I'm sure thou cassen –
But that the squier, or the pa'son,
Mid be our friend, Tom, after all?
The times be hard, 'tis true! an' they that got
210 His blessèns, shoulden let theirzelves vorget
How 'tis where vo'k do never zet
A bit o' meat within their rusty pot.
The man a-zittèn in his easy chair
To flesh, an' vowl, an' vish, should try to speäre
The poor theäse times, a little vrom his store;
An' if he don't, why sin is at his door.

TOM
Ah! we won't look to that; we'll have our right, –
If not by feäre meäns, then we wull by might.
We'll meäke times better vor us; we'll be free
220 Ov other vo'k an' others' charity.

JOHN
Ah! I do think you mid as well be quiet;
You'll meäke things wo'se, i'-ma'-be, by a riot.
You'll get into a mess, Tom, I'm afeärd;
You'll goo vor wool, an' then come hwome a-sheär'd.

Second Collection

(Originally *Hwomely Rhymes*, 1859)

My Orcha'd in Linden Lea

'Ithin the woodlands, flow'ry gleäded,
By the woak tree's mossy moot,
The sheenèn grass-bleädes, timber-sheäded,
Now do quiver under voot;
An' birds do whissle over head,
An' water's bubblèn in its bed,
An' there vor me the apple tree
Do leän down low in Linden Lea.

When leaves that leätely wer a-springèn
10 Now do feäde 'ithin the copse,
An' païnted birds do hush their zingèn
Up upon the timber's tops;
An' brown-leav'd fruit's a-turnèn red,
In cloudless zunsheen, over head,
Wi' fruit vor me, the apple tree
Do leän down low in Linden Lea.

Let other vo'k meäke money vaster
In the aïr o' dark-room'd towns,
I don't dread a peevish meäster;
20 Though noo man do heed my frowns,
I be free to goo abrode,
Or teäke ageän my hwomeward road
To where, vor me, the apple tree
Do leän down low in Linden Lea.

Ellen Brine ov Allenburn

Noo soul did hear her lips complain,
An' she's a-gone vrom all her païn,
An' others' loss to her is gaïn
Vor she do live in heaven's love;
Vull many a longsome day an' week
She bore her aïlèn, still, an' meek;
A-workèn while her strangth held on,
An' guidèn housework, when 'twer gone.
Vor Ellen Brine ov Allenburn,
10 Oh! there be souls to murn.

The last time I'd a-cast my zight
Upon her feäce, a-feäded white,
Wer in a zummer's mornèn light
In hall avore the smwold'rèn vier,
The while the childern beät the vloor,
In plaÿ, wi' tiny shoes they wore,
An' call'd their mother's eyes to view
The feäts their little limbs could do.
Oh! Ellen Brine ov Allenburn,
20 They childern now mus' murn.

Then woone, a-stoppèn vrom his reäce,
Went up, an' on her knee did pleäce
His hand, a-lookèn in her feäce,
An' wi' a smilèn mouth so small,
He zaid, 'You promised us to goo
To Shroton feäir, an teäke us two!'
She heärd it wi' her two white ears,
An' in her eyes there sprung two tears,
Vor Ellen Brine ov Allenburn
30 Did veel that they mus' murn.

September come, wi' Shroton feäir,
But Ellen Brine wer never there!
A heavy heart wer on the meäre
Their father rod his hwomeward road.

'Tis true he brought zome feärèns back,
Vor them two childern all in black;
But they had now, wi' plaÿthings new,
Noo mother vor to shew em to,
Vor Ellen Brine ov Allenburn
40 Would never mwore return.

The Leädy's Tower

An' then we went along the gleädes
O' zunny turf, in quiv'ren sheädes,
A-windèn off, vrom hand to hand,
Along a path o' yollow zand,
An' clomb a stickle slope, an' vound
An open patch o' lofty ground,
Up where a steätely tow'r did spring,
So high as highest larks do zing.

'Oh! Meäster Collins,' then I zaid,
10 A-lookèn up wi' back-flung head;
Vor who but he, so mild o' feäce,
Should teäke me there to zee the pleäce.
'What is it then theäse tower do meän,
A-built so feäir, an' kept so cleän?'
'Ah! me,' he zaid, wi' thoughtvul feäce,
''Twer grief that zet theäse tower in pleäce.
The squier's e'thly life's a-blest
Wi' gifts that mwost do teäke vor best;
The lofty-pinion'd rufs do rise
20 To screen his head vrom stormy skies;
His land's a-spreadèn roun' his hall,
An' hands do leäbor at his call;
The while the ho'se do fling, wi' pride,
His lofty head where he do guide;
But still his e'thly jaÿ's a-vled,
His woone true friend, his wife, is dead.

Zoo now her happy soul's a-gone,
An' he in grief's a-ling'rèn on,
Do do his heart zome good to show
30 His love to flesh an' blood below.
An' zoo he rear'd, wi' smitten soul,
Theäse Leädy's Tower upon the knowl.
An' there you'll zee the tow'r do spring
Twice ten veet up, as roun's a ring,
Wi' pillars under mwolded eäves,
Above their heads a-carv'd wi' leäves;
An' have to peäce, a-walkèn round
His voot, a hunderd veet o' ground.
An' there, above his upper wall,
40 A roundèd tow'r do spring so tall
'S a springèn arrow shot upright,
A hunderd giddy veet in height.
An' if you'd like to straïn your knees
A-climèn up above the trees,
To zee, wi' slowly wheelèn feäce,
The vur-sky'd land about the pleäce,
You'll have a flight o' steps to wear
Vor forty veet, up steäir by steäir,
That roun' the risèn tow'r do wind,
50 Like withwind roun' the saplèn's rind,
An' reach a landèn, wi' a seat,
To rest at last your weary veet,
'Ithin a breast be-screenèn wall,
To keep ye vrom a longsome vall.
An' roun' the windèn steäirs do spring
Aïght stwonèn pillars in a ring,
A-reachèn up their heavy strangth
Drough forty veet o' slender langth,
To end wi' carvèd heads below
60 The broad-vloor'd landèn's aïry bow.
Aïght zides, as you do zee, do bound
The lower buildèn on the ground,
An' there in woone, a two-leav'd door
Do zwing above the marble vloor:

An' aÿe, as luck do zoo betide
Our comèn, we can goo inside.
The door is open now. An' zoo
The keeper kindly let us drough.
There as we softly trod the vloor
70 O' marble stwone, 'ithin the door,
The echoes ov our vootsteps vled
Out roun' the wall, and over head;
An' there a-païnted, zide by zide,
In memory o' the squier's bride,
In zeven païntèns, true to life,
Wer zeven zights o' wedded life.'

Then Meäster Collins twold me all
The teäles a-païntèd roun' the wall;
An' vu'st the bride did stan' to plight
80 Her weddèn vow, below the light
A-shootèn down, so bright's a fleäme,
In drough a churches window freäme.
An' near the bride, on either hand,
You'd zee her comely bridemaïds stand,
Wi' eyelashes a-bent in streäks
O' brown above their bloomèn cheäks:
An' sheenèn feäir, in mellow light,
Wi' flowèn heäir, an' frocks o' white.

'An' here,' good Meäster Collins cried,
90 'You'll zee a creädle at her zide,
An' there's her child, a-lyèn deep
'Ithin it an' a-gone to sleep,
Wi' little eyelashes a-met
In fellow streäks, as black as jet;
The while her needle, over head,
Do nimbly leäd the snow-white thread,
To zew a robe her love do meäke
Wi' happy leäbor vor his seäke.

'An' here ageän's another pleäce,
100 Where she do zit wi' smilèn feäce,

An' while her bwoy do leän, wi' pride,
Ageän her lap, below her zide,
Her vinger tip do leäd his look
To zome good words o' God's own book.

'An' next you'll zee her in her pleäce,
Avore her happy husband's feäce,
As he do zit, at evenèn-tide,
A-restèn by the vier-zide.
An' there the childern's heads do rise,
110 Wi' laughèn lips, an' beamèn eyes,
Above the bwoard, where she do lay
Her sheenèn tacklèn, wi' the tea.

'An' here another zide do show
Her vinger in her scizzars' bow
Avore two daughters, that do stand,
Wi' leärnsome minds, to watch her hand
A-sheäpèn out, wi' skill an' ceäre,
A frock vor them to zew an' wear.

'Then next you'll zee her bend her head
120 Above her aïlèn husband's bed,
A-fannèn, wi' an inward praÿ'r,
His burnèn brow wi' beäten aïr;
The while the clock, by candle light,
Do show that 'tis the dead o' night.

'An' here ageän upon the wall,
Where we do zee her last ov all,
Her husband's head's a-hangèn low,
'Ithin his hands in deepest woe.
An' she, an angel ov his God,
130 Do cheer his soul below the rod,
A-liftèn up her han' to call
His eyes to writèn on the wall,
As white as is her spotless robe,
"Hast thou rememberèd my servant Job?"

'An' zoo the squier, in grief o' soul,
Built up the Tower upon the knowl.'

Childhood

Aye, at that time our days wer but vew,
An' our lim's wer but small, an' a-growèn;
An' then the feäir worold wer new,
An' life wer all hopevul an' gaÿ;
An' the times o' the sproutèn o' leaves,
An' the cheäk-burnèn seasons o' mowèn,
An' bindèn o' red-headed sheaves,
Wer all welcome seasons o' jaÿ.

Then the housen seem'd high, that be low,
10 An' the brook did seem wide that is narrow,
An' time, that do vlee, did goo slow,
An' veelèns now feeble wer strong,
An' our worold did end wi' the neämes
Ov the Sha'sbury Hill or Bulbarrow;
An' life did seem only the geämes
That we plaÿ'd as the days rolled along.

Then the rivers, an' high-timber'd lands,
An' the zilvery hills, 'ithout buyèn,
Did seem to come into our hands
20 Vrom others that own'd em avore;
An' all zickness, an' sorrow, an' need,
Seem'd to die wi' the wold vo'k a-dyèn,
An' leäve us vor ever a-freed
Vrom evils our vorefathers bore.

But happy be childern the while
They have elders a-livèn to love em,
An' teäke all the wearisome tweil
That zome hands or others mus' do;
Like the low-headed shrubs that be warm,
30 In the lewth o' the trees up above em,
A-screen'd vrom the cwold blowèn storm
That the timber avore em must rue.

Meäry's Smile

When mornèn winds, a-blowèn high,
Do zweep the clouds vrom all the sky,
An' laurel-leaves do glitter bright,
The while the newly broken light
Do brighten up, avore our view,
The vields wi' green, an' hills wi' blue;
What then can highten to my eyes
The cheerful feäce ov e'th an' skies,
But Meäry's smile, o' Morey's Mill,
10 My rwose o' Mowy Lea.

An' when, at last, the evenèn dews
Do now begin to wet our shoes;
An' night's a-ridèn to the west,
To stop our work, an' gi'e us rest,
Oh! let the candle's ruddy gleäre
But brighten up her sheenèn heäir;
Or else, as she do walk abroad,
Let moonlight show, upon the road,
My Meäry's smile, o' Morey's Mill,
20 My rwose o' Mowy Lea.

An' O! mid never tears come on,
To wash her feäce's blushes wan,
Nor kill her smiles that now do plaÿ
Like sparklèn weäves in zunny Maÿ;
But mid she still, vor all she's gone
Vrom souls she now do smile upon,
Show others they can vind woone jaÿ
To turn the hardest work to plaÿ.
My Meäry's smile, o' Morey's Mill,
30 My rwose o' Mowy Lea.

Meäry Wedded

The zun can zink, the stars mid rise,
An' woods be green to sheenèn skies;
The cock mid crow to mornèn light,
An' workvo'k zing to vallèn night;
The birds mid whissle on the spraÿ,
An' childern leäp in merry plaÿ,
But our's is now a lifeless pleäce,
Vor we've a-lost a smilèn feäce –
  Young Meäry Meäd o' merry mood,
10 Vor she's a-woo'd an' wedded.

The dog that woonce wer glad to bear
Her fondlèn vingers down his heäir,
Do leän his head ageän the vloor,
To watch, wi' heavy eyes, the door;
An' men she zent so happy hwome
O' Zadurdays, do seem to come
To door, wi' downcast hearts, to miss
Wi' smiles below the clematis,
  Young Meäry Meäd o' merry mood,
20 Vor she's a-woo'd an' wedded.

When they do draw the evenèn blind,
An' when the evenèn light's a-tin'd,
The cheerless vier do drow a gleäre
O' light ageän her empty chair;
An' wordless gaps do now meäke thin
Their talk where woonce her vaïce come in.
Zoo lwonesome is her empty pleäce,
An' blest the house that ha' the feäce
  O' Meäry Meäd o' merry mood,
30 Now she's a-woo'd an' wedded.

The day she left her father's he'th,
Though sad, wer kept a day o' me'th,

An' dry-wheel'd waggons' empty beds
Wer left 'ithin the tree-screen'd sheds;
An' all the hosses, at their eäse,
Went snortèn up the flow'ry leäse,
But woone, the smartest vor the roäd,
That pull'd away the dearest lwoad –
  Young Meäry Meäd o' merry mood,
40 That wer a-woo'd an' wedded.

The Young that Died in Beauty

If souls should only sheen so bright
In heaven as in e'thly light,
An' nothèn better wer the ceäse,
How comely still, in sheäpe an' feäce,
Would many reach thik happy pleäce, –
The hopevul souls that in their prime
Ha' seem'd a-took avore their time, –
The young that died in beauty.

But when woone's lim's ha' lost their strength
10 A-tweilèn drough a lifetime's langth,
An' over cheäks a-growèn wold
The slowly-weästèn years ha' roll'd
The deep'nèn wrinkle's hollow vwold;
When life is ripe, then death do call
Vor less ov thought, than when do vall
On young vo'ks in their beauty.

But pinèn souls, wi' heads a-hung
In heavy sorrow vor the young,
The sister ov the brother dead,
20 The father wi' a child a-vled,
The husband when his bride ha' laid
Her head at rest, noo mwore to turn,
Have all a-vound the time to murn
Vor youth that died in beauty.

An' yeet the church, where praÿer do rise
Vrom thoughtvul souls, wi' downcast eyes,
An' village greens, a-beät half beäre
By dancers that do meet, an' weär
Such merry looks at feäst an' feäir,
30 Do gather under leätest skies,
Their bloomèn cheäks an' sparklèn eyes,
Though young ha' died in beauty.

But still the dead shall mwore than keep
The beauty ov their eärly sleep;
Where comely looks shall never weär
Uncomely, under tweil an' ceäre.
The feäir at death be always feäir,
Still feäir to livers' thought an' love,
An' feäirer still to God above,
40 Than when they died in beauty.

Minden House

'Twer when the vo'k wer out to hawl
A vield o' haÿ a daÿ in June,
An' when the zun begun to vall
Toward the west in afternoon,
Woone only wer a-left behind
To bide indoors, at hwome, an' mind
The house, an' answer vo'k avore
The geäte or door, – young Fanny Deäne.

The aïr 'ithin the geärden wall
10 Wer deadly still, unless the bee
Did hummy by, or in the hall
The clock did ring a-hettèn dree,
An' there, wi' busy hands, inside
The iron ceäsement, open'd wide,
Did zit an' pull wi' nimble twitch
Her tiny stitch, young Fanny Deäne.

As there she zot she heärd two blows
A-knock'd upon the rumblèn door,
An' laid azide her work, an' rose,
20 An' walk'd out feäir, athirt the vloor;
An' there, a-holdèn in his hand
His bridled meäre, a youth did stand,
An' mildly twold his neäme and pleäce
Avore the feäce o' Fanny Deäne.

He twold her that he had on hand
Zome business on his father's zide,
But what she didden understand;
An' zoo she ax'd en if he'd ride
Out where her father mid be vound,
30 Bezide the plow, in Cowslip Ground;
An' there he went, but left his mind
Back there behind, wi' Fanny Deäne.

Ah' oh! his hwomeward road wer gaÿ
In aïr a-blowèn, whiff by whiff,
While sheenèn water-weäves did plaÿ
An' boughs did swaÿ above the cliff;
Vor Time had now a-show'd en dim
The jaÿ it had in store vor him;
An' when he went thik road ageän
40 His errand then wer Fanny Deäne.

How strangely things be brought about
By Providence, noo tongue can tell.
She minded house, when vo'k wer out,
An' zoo mus' bid the house farewell;
The bees mid hum, the clock mid call
The lwonesome hours 'ithin the hall,
But in behind the woaken door,
There's now noo mwore a Fanny Deäne.

Our Be'thpleäce

How dear's the door a latch do shut,
An' geärden that a hatch do shut,
Where vu'st our bloomèn cheäks ha'prest
The pillor ov our childhood's rest;
Or where, wi' little tooes, we wore
The paths our fathers trod avore;
Or clim'd the timber's bark aloft,
Below the zingèn lark aloft,
The while we heärd the echo sound
10 Drough all the ringèn valley round.

A lwonesome grove o' woak did rise,
To screen our house, where smoke did rise,
A-twistèn blue, while yeet the zun
Did langthen on our childhood's fun;
An' there, wi' all the sheäpes an' sounds
O' life, among the timber'd grounds,
The birds upon their boughs did zing,
An' milkmaïds by their cows did zing,
Wi' merry sounds, that softly died,
20 A-ringèn down the valley zide.

By river banks, wi' reeds a-bound,
An' sheenèn pools, wi' weeds a-bound,
The long-neck'd gander's ruddy bill
To snow-white geese did cackle sh'ill;
An' stridèn peewits heästen'd by,
O' tiptooe wi' their screamèn cry;
An' stalkèn cows a-lowèn loud,
An' struttèn cocks a-crowèn loud,
Did rouse the echoes up to mock
30 Their mingled sounds by hill an' rock.

The stars that clim'd our skies all dark,
Above our sleepèn eyes all dark,
An' zuns a-rollèn round to bring
The seasons on, vrom Spring to Spring,

Ha' vled, wi' never-restèn flight,
Drough green-bough'd day, an' dark-tree'd night;
Till now our childhood's pleäces there,
Be gaÿ wi' other feäces there,
An' we ourselves do vollow on
40 Our own vorelivers dead an' gone.

Slow to Come, Quick a-Gone

Ah! there's a house that I do know
Besouth o' yonder trees,
Where northern winds can hardly blow
But in a softest breeze.
An' there woonce sounded zongs an' teäles
Vrom vaïce o' maïd or youth,
An' sweeter than the nightèngeäle's
Above the copses lewth.

How swiftly there did run the brooks,
10 How swift wer winds in flight,
How swiftly to their roost the rooks
Did vlee o'er head at night.
Though slow did seem to us the peäce
O' comèn days a-head,
That now do seem as in a reäce
Wi' aïr-birds to ha' vled.

The Wold Wall

Here, Jeäne, we vu'st did meet below
The leafy boughs, a-swingèn slow,
Avore the zun, wi' evenèn glow,
Above our road, a-beamèn red;
The grass in zwath wer in the meäds,
The water gleam'd among the reeds

In aïr a-steälèn roun' the hall,
Where ivy clung upon the wall.
Ah! well-a-day! O wall adieu!
10 The wall is wold, my grief is new.

An' there you walk'd wi' blushèn pride,
Where softly-wheelèn streams did glide,
Drough sheädes o' poplars at my zide,
An' there wi' love that still do live,
Your feäce did wear the smile o' youth,
The while you spoke wi' age's truth,
An' wi' a rwosebud's mossy ball,
I deck'd your bosom vrom the wall.
Ah! well-a-day! O wall adieu!
20 The wall is wold, my grief is new.

But now when winter's raïn do vall,
An' wind do beät ageän the hall,
The while upon the wat'ry wall
In spots o' grey the moss do grow,
The ruf noo mwore shall overspread
The pillor ov our weary head,
Nor shall the rwose's mossy ball
Behang vor you the house's wall.
Ah! well-a-day! O wall adieu!
30 The wall is wold, my grief is new.

Zun-zet

Where the western zun, unclouded,
  Up above the grey hill-tops,
Did sheen drough ashes, lofty sh'ouded,
  On the turf bezide the copse,
    In zummer weather,
    We together,
    Sorrow-slightèn, work-vorgettèn,
    Gambol'd wi' the zun a-zettèn.

There, by flow'ry bows o' bramble,
10 Under hedge, in ash-tree sheädes,
The dun-heaïr'd ho'se did slowly ramble
On the grasses' dewy bleädes,
Zet free o' lwoads,
An' stwony rwoads,
Vorgetvul o' the lashes frettèn,
Grazèn wi' the zun a-zettèn.

There wer rooks a-beätèn by us
Drough the aïr, in a vlock,
An' there the lively blackbird, nigh us,
20 On the meäple bough did rock,
Wi' ringèn droat,
Where zunlight smote
The yollow boughs o' zunny hedges
Over western hills' blue edges.

Waters, drough the meäds a-purlèn,
Glissen'd in the evenèn's light,
An' smoke, above the town a-curlèn,
Melted slowly out o' zight;
An' there, in glooms
30 Ov unzunn'd rooms,
To zome, wi' idle sorrows frettèn,
Zuns did zet avore their zettèn.

We were out in geämes and reäces,
Loud a-laughèn, wild in me'th,
Wi' windblown heäir, an' zunbrown'd feäces,
Leäpèn on the high-sky'd e'th,
Avore the lights
Wer tin'd o' nights,
An' while the gossamer's light nettèn
40 Sparkled to the zun a-zettèn.

The Water Crowvoot

O small-feäc'd flow'r that now dost bloom
To stud wi' white the shallow Frome,
An' leäve the clote to spread his flow'r
On darksome pools o' stwoneless Stour,
When sof'ly-rizèn aïrs do cool
The water in the sheenèn pool,
Thy beds o' snow-white buds do gleam
So feäir upon the sky-blue stream,
As whitest clouds, a-hangèn high
10 Avore the blueness o' the sky;
An' there, at hand, the thin-heäir'd cows,
In aïry sheädes o' withy boughs,
Or up bezide the mossy raïls,
Do stan' an' zwing their heavy taïls,
The while the ripplèn stream do flow
Below the dousty bridge's bow;
An' quiv'rèn water-gleams do mock
The weäves, upon the sheäded rock;
An' up athirt the copèn stwone
20 The laïtren bwoy do leän alwone,
A-watchèn, wi' a stedvast look,
The vallèn waters in the brook,
The while the zand o' time do run
An' leäve his errand still undone.
An' oh! as long's thy buds would gleam
Above the softly-slidèn stream,
While sparklèn zummer-brooks do run
Below the lofty-climèn zun,
I only wish that thou could'st staÿ
30 Vor noo man's harm, an' all men's jaÿ.
But no, the waterman 'ull weäde
Thy water wi' his deadly bleäde,
To slaÿ thee even in thy bloom,
Fair small-feäc'd flow'r o' the Frome.

The Leäne

They do zay that a travellèn chap
   Have a-put in the newspeäper now,
That the bit o' green ground on the knap
   Should be all a-took in vor the plough.
He do fancy 'tis easy to show
   That we can be but stunpolls at best,
Vor to leäve a green spot where a flower can grow,
   Or a voot-weary walker mid rest.
'Tis hedge-grubbèn, Thomas, an' ledge-grubbèn,
10   Never a-done
While a sov'rèn mwore's to be won.

The road, he do zay, is so wide
   As 'tis wanted vor travellers' wheels,
As if all that did travel did ride,
   An' did never get galls on their heels.
He would leäve sich a thin strip o' groun',
   That, if a man's veet in his shoes
Wer a-burnèn an' zore, why he coulden zit down
   But the wheels would run over his tooes.
20 Vor 'tis meäke money, Thomas, an' teäke money,
      What's zwold an' bought
Is all that is worthy o' thought.

Years agoo the leäne-zides did bear grass,
   Vor to pull wi' the geeses' red bills,
That did hiss at the vo'k that did pass,
   Or the bwoys that pick'd up their white quills.
But shortly, if vower or vive
   Ov our goslèns do creep vrom the agg,
They must mwope in the geärden, mwore dead than alive,
30 In a coop, or a-tied by the lag.
Vor to catch at land, Thomas, an' snatch at land,
      Now is the plan;
Meäke money wherever you can.

The childern wull soon have noo pleäce
  Vor to plaÿ in, an' if they do grow,
They wull have a thin musheroom feäce,
  Wi' their bodies so sumple as dough.
But a man is a-meäde ov a child,
  An' his limbs do grow worksome by plaÿ;
40 An' if the young child's little body's a-spweil'd,
  Why, the man's wull the sooner decaÿ.
But wealth is wo'th now mwore than health is wo'th;
    Let it all goo,
If 't 'ull bring but a sov'rèn or two.

Vor to breed the young fox or the heäre,
  We can gi'e up whole eäcres o' ground,
But the greens be a-grudg'd, vor to rear
  Our young childern up healthy an' sound;
Why, there woon't be a-left the next age
50 A green spot where their veet can goo free;
An' the gookoo wull soon be committed to cage
  Vor a trespass in zomebody's tree.
Vor 'tis lockèn up, Thomas, an' blockèn up,
    Stranger or brother,
Men mussen come nigh woone another.

Woone day I went in at a geäte,
  Wi' my child, where an echo did sound,
An' the owner come up, an' did reäte
  Me as if I would car off his ground.
60 But his vield an' the grass wer a-let,
  An' the damage that he could a-took
Wer at mwost that the while I did open the geäte
  I did rub roun' the eye on the hook.
But 'tis drevèn out, Thomas, an' hevèn out.
    Trample noo grounds,
Unless you be after the hounds.

Ah! the Squier o' Culver-dell Hall
  Wer as diff'rent as light is vrom dark,
Wi' zome vo'k that, as evenèn did vall,
70 Had a-broke drough long grass in his park;

Vor he went, wi' a smile, vor to meet
  Wi' the trespassers while they did pass,
An' he zaid, 'I do fear you'll catch cwold in your veet,
  You've a-walk'd drough so much o' my grass.'
His mild words, Thomas, cut 'em like swords, Thomas,
    Newly a-whet,
An' went vurder wi' them than a dreat.

Trees be Company

When zummer's burnèn het's a-shed
Upon the droopèn grasses head,
A-drevèn under sheädy leaves
The workvo'k in their snow-white sleeves,
We then mid yearn to clim' the height,
  Where thorns be white, above the vern;
An' aïr do turn the zunsheen's might
  To softer light too weak to burn –
    On woodless downs we mid be free,
10   But lowland trees be company.

Though downs mid show a wider view
O' green a-reachèn into blue
Than roads a-windèn in the glen,
An' ringèn wi' the sounds o' men;
The thissle's crown o' red an' blue
  In Fall's cwold dew do wither brown,
An' larks come down 'ithin the lew,
  As storms do brew, an' skies do frown –
    An' though the down do let us free,
20   The lowland trees be company.

Where birds do zing, below the zun,
In trees above the blue-smok'd tun,
An' sheädes o' stems do overstratch
The mossy path 'ithin the hatch;

If leaves be bright up over head,
When Maÿ do shed its glitt'rèn light;
Or, in the blight o' Fall, do spread
A yollow bed avore our zight –
Whatever season it mid be,
30 The trees be always company.

When dusky night do nearly hide
The path along the hedge's zide,
An' daylight's hwomely sounds be still
But sounds o' water at the mill;
Then if noo feäce we long'd to greet
Could come to meet our lwonesome treäce
Or if noo peäce o' weary veet,
However fleet, could reach its pleäce –
However lwonesome we mid be,
40 The trees would still be company.

False Friends-like

When I wer still a bwoy, an' mother's pride,
A bigger bwoy spoke up to me so kind-like,
'If you do like, I'll treat ye wi' a ride
In theäse wheel-barrow here.' Zoo I wer blind-like
To what he had a-workèn in his mind-like,
An' mounted vor a passenger inside;
An' comèn to a puddle, perty wide,
He tipp'd me in, a-grinnèn back behind-like.
Zoo when a man do come to me so thick-like,
10 An' sheäke my hand, where woonce he pass'd me by,
An' tell me he would do me this or that,
I can't help thinkèn o' the big bwoy's trick-like.
An' then, vor all I can but wag my hat
An' thank en, I do veel a little shy.

The Wife a-Lost

Since I noo mwore do zee your feäce,
Up steäirs or down below,
I'll zit me in the lwonesome pleäce,
Where flat-bough'd beech do grow;
Below the beeches' bough, my love,
Where you did never come,
An' I don't look to meet ye now,
As I do look at hwome.

Since you noo mwore be at my zide,
10 In walks in zummer het,
I'll goo alwone where mist do ride,
Drough trees a-drippèn wet;
Below the raïn-wet bough, my love,
Where you did never come,
An' I don't grieve to miss ye now,
As I do grieve at hwome

Since now bezide my dinner-bwoard
Your vaïce do never sound,
I'll eat the bit I can avword,
20 A-vield upon the ground;
Below the darksome bough, my love,
Where you did never dine,
An' I don't grieve to miss ye now,
As I at hwome do pine.

Since I do miss your vaïce an' feäce
In praÿer at eventide,
I'll praÿ wi' woone sad vaïce vor greäce
To goo where you do bide;
Above the tree an' bough, my love,
30 Where you be gone avore,
An' be a-waïtèn vor me now,
To come vor evermwore.

The Bwoat

Where cows did slowly seek the brink
O' Stour, drough zunburnt grass, to drink;
Wi' vishèn float, that there did zink
An' rise, I zot as in a dream.
The dazzlèn zun did cast his light
On hedge-row blossom, snowy white,
Though nothèn yet did come in zight,
A-stirrèn on the straÿèn stream;

Till, out by sheädy rocks there show'd,
10 A bwoat along his foamy road,
Wi' thik feäir maïd at mill, a-row'd
Wi' Jeäne behind her brother's oars.
An' steätely as a queen o' vo'k,
She zot wi' floatèn scarlet cloak,
An' comèn on, at ev'ry stroke,
Between my withy-sheäded shores.

The broken stream did idly try
To show her sheäpe a-ridèn by,
The rushes brown-bloom'd stems did ply,
20 As if they bow'd to her by will.
The rings o' water, wi' a sock,
Did break upon the mossy rock,
An' gi'e my beätèn heart a shock,
Above my float's up-leäpèn quill.

Then, lik' a cloud below the skies,
A-drifted off, wi' less'nèn size,
An' lost, she floated vrom my eyes,
Where down below the stream did wind;
An' left the quiet weäves woonce mwore
30 To zink to rest, a sky-blue'd vloor,
Wi' all so still's the clote they bore,
Aye, all but my own ruffled mind.

Pentridge by the River

Pentridge! – oh! my heart's a-zwellèn
Vull o' jaÿ wi' vo'k a-tellèn
  Any news o' thik wold pleäce,
An' the boughy hedges round it,
An' the river that do bound it
  Wi' his dark but glis'nèn feäce.
Vor there's noo land, on either hand,
To me lik' Pentridge by the river.

Be there any leaves to quiver
10 On the aspen by the river?
  Doo he sheäde the water still,
Where the rushes be a-growèn,
Where the sullen Stour's a-flowèn
  Drough the meäds vrom mill to mill?
Vor if a tree wer dear to me,
Oh! 'twer thik aspen by the river.

There, in eegrass new a-shootèn,
I did run on even vootèn,
  Happy, over new-mow'd land;
20 Or did zing wi' zingèn drushes
While I plaïted, out o' rushes,
  Little baskets vor my hand;
Bezide the clote that there did float,
Wi' yollow blossoms, on the river.

When the western zun's a-vallèn,
What sh'ill vaïce is now a-callèn
  Hwome the deäiry to the païls;
Who do dreve em on, a-flingèn
Wide-bow'd horns, or slowly zwingèn
30 Right an' left their tufty taïls?
As they do goo a-huddled drough
The geäte a-leädèn up vrom river.

Bleäded grass is now a-shootèn
Where the vloor wer woonce our vootèn,

While the hall wer still in pleäce.
Stwones be looser in the wallèn;
Hollow trees be nearer vallèn;
Ev'ry thing ha' chang'd its feäce.
But still the neäme do bide the seäme –
40 'Tis Pentridge – Pentridge by the river.

Happiness

Ah! you do seem to think the ground,
Where happiness is best a-vound,
Is where the high-peäl'd park do reach
Wi' elem-rows, or clumps o' beech,
Or where the coach do stand avore
The twelve-tunn'd house's lofty door,
Or men can ride behin' their hounds
Vor miles athirt their own wide grounds,
An' seldom wi' the lowly;
10 Upon the green that we do tread,
Below the welsh-nut's wide-limb'd head,
Or grass where apple trees do spread?
No, so's; no, no: not high nor low:
'Tis where the heart is holy.

'Tis true its veet mid tread the vloor,
'Ithin the marble-pillar'd door,
Where day do cast, in high-ruf'd halls,
His light drough lofty window'd walls;
An' wax-white han's do never tire
20 Wi' strokes ov heavy work vor hire,
An' all that money can avword
Do lwoad the zilver-brighten'd bwoard;
Or mid be wi' the lowly,
Where turf's a-smwolderèn avore
The back, to warm the stwonèn vloor,
An' love's at hwome 'ithin the door?
No, so's; no, no: not high nor low:
'Tis where the heart is holy.

An' ceäre can come 'ithin a ring
30 O' sworded guards, to smite a king,
Though he mid hold 'ithin his hands
The zwarmèn vo'k o' many lands;
Or goo in drough the iron-geäte
Avore the house o' lofty steäte;
Or reach the miser that do smile
A-buildèn up his goolden pile;
Or else mid smite the lowly,
That have noo pow'r to loose or bind
Another's body, or his mind,
40 But only hands to help mankind.
If there is rest 'ithin the breast,
'Tis where the heart is holy.

My Love's Guardian Angel

As in the cool-aïr'd road I come by,
– in the night,
Under the moon-clim'd height o' the sky,
– in the night,
There by the lime's broad lim's as I staÿ'd,
Dark in the moonlight, bough's sheädows plaÿ'd
Up on the window-glass that did keep
Lew vrom the wind, my true love asleep,
– in the night.

10 While in the grey-wall'd height o' the tow'r,
– in the night,
Sounded the midnight bell wi' the hour,
– in the night,
There lo! a bright-heäir'd angel that shed
Light vrom her white robe's zilvery thread,
Put her vore-vinger up vor to meäke
Silence around lest sleepers mid weäke,
– in the night.

'Oh! then,' I whisper'd, 'do I behold
20 – in the night,
Linda, my true-love, here in the cwold,
– in the night?'
'No,' she meäde answer, 'you do misteäke:
She is asleep, but I that do weäke,
Here be on watch, an angel a-blest,
Over her slumber while she do rest,
– in the night.

'Zee how the winds, while here by the bough,
– in the night,
30 They do pass on, don't smite on her brow,
– in the night;
Zee how the cloud-sheädes naïseless do zweep
Over the house-top where she's asleep.
You, too, goo by, in times that be near,
You too, as I, mid speak in her ear
– in the night.'

Third Collection

(Originally *Poems of Rural Life in the Dorset Dialect*, 1862)

Woone Smile Mwore

O! Meäry, when the zun went down,
  Woone night in Spring, wi' vi'ry rim,
Behind thik knap wi' woody crown,
  An' left your smilèn feäce so dim;
Your little sister there, inside,
  Wi' bellows on her little knee,
Did blow the vier, a-gleärèn wide
  Drough window-peänes, that I could zee, –
As you did stan' wi' me, avore
10 The house, a-peärtèn, – woone smile mwore.

The chatt'rèn birds, a-risèn high,
  An' zinkèn low, did swiftly vlee
Vrom shrinken moss a-growèn dry,
  Upon the leänèn apple tree.
An' there the dog, a-whippèn wide
  His heäiry taïl, an' comèn near,
Did fondly lay ageän your zide
  His coal-black nose an' russet ear:
To win what I'd a-won avore,
20 Vrom your gaÿ feäce, his woone smile mwore.

An' while your mother bustled sprack,
  A-gettèn supper out in hall,
An' cast her sheäde, a-whiv'rèn black
  Avore the vier, upon the wall;
Your brother come, wi' easy peäce,
  In drough the slammèn geäte, along
The path, wi' healthy-bloomèn feäce,
  A-whis'lèn shrill his last new zong;

An' when he come avore the door,
30 He met vrom you his woone smile mwore.

Now you that wer the daughter there,
Be mother on a husband's vloor,
An' mid ye meet wi' less o' ceäre
Than what your hearty mother bore;
An' if abroad I have to rue
The bitter tongue, or wrongvul deed,
Mid I come hwome to sheäre wi' you
What's needvul free o' pinchèn need:
An' vind that you ha' still in store,
40 My evenèn meal, an' woone smile mwore.

The Lark

As I, below the mornèn sky,
Wer out a-workèn in the lew
O' black-stemm'd thorns, a-springèn high,
Avore the worold-boundèn blue,
A-reäkèn, under woak tree boughs,
The orts a-left behin' by cows.

Above the grey-grow'd thistle rings,
An' deäisy-buds, the lark, in flight,
Did zing aloft, wi' flappèn wings,
10 Tho' mwore in heärèn than in zight;
The while my bwoys, in plaÿvul me'th,
Did run till they wer out o' breath.

Then woone, wi' han'-besheäded eyes,
A-stoppèn still, as he did run,
Look'd up to zee the lark arise
A-zingèn to the high-gone zun;
The while his brother look'd below
Vor what the groun' mid have to show.

Zoo woone did watch above his head
20 The bird his hands could never teäke;
An' woone, below, where he did tread,
Vound out the nest within the breäke;
But, aggs be only woonce a-vound,
An' uncaught larks ageän mid sound.

Woak Hill

When sycamore leaves wer a-spreadèn,
Green-ruddy, in hedges,
Bezide the red doust o' the ridges,
A-dried at Woak Hill;

I packed up my goods all a-sheenèn
Wi' long years o' handlèn,
On dousty red wheels ov a waggon,
To ride at Woak Hill.

The brown thatchen ruf o' the dwellèn
10 I then wer a-leävèn,
Had shelter'd the sleek head o' Meäry,
My bride at Woak Hill.

But now vor zome years, her light voot-vall
'S a-lost vrom the vloorèn.
Too soon vor my jaÿ an' my childern,
She died at Woak Hill.

But still I do think that, in soul,
She do hover about us;
To ho vor her motherless childern,
20 Her pride at Woak Hill.

Zoo – lest she should tell me hereafter
I stole off 'ithout her,
An' left her, uncall'd at house-riddèn,
To bide at Woak Hill –

I call'd her so fondly, wi' lippèns
  All soundless to others,
An' took her wi' aïr-reachèn hand,
  To my zide at Woak Hill.

On the road I did look round, a-talkèn
30 To light at my shoulder,
An' then led her in at the door-way,
  Miles wide vrom Woak Hill.

An' that's why vo'k thought, vor a season,
  My mind wer a-wandrèn
Wi' sorrow, when I wer so sorely
  A-tried at Woak Hill.

But no; that my Meäry mid never
  Behold herzelf slighted,
I wanted to think that I guided
40 My guide vrom Woak Hill.

Pickèn o' Scroff

Oh! the wood wer a-vell'd in the copse,
  An' the moss-bedded primrwose did blow;
An' vrom tall-stemmèd trees' leafless tops,
  There did lie but slight sheädes down below.
An' the sky wer a-showèn, in drough
By the tree-stems, the deepest o' blue,
Wi' a light that did vall on an' off
The dry ground, a-strew'd over wi' scroff.

There the hedge that were leätely so high,
10 Wer a-plush'd, an' along by the zide,
Where the waggon 'd a-haul'd the wood by,
  There did reach the deep wheelrouts, a-dried.
An' the groun' wi' the sticks wer bespread,
Zome a-cut off alive, an' zome dead,
An' vor burnèn, well wo'th reäkèn off,
By the childern a-pickèn o' scroff.

In the tree-studded leäze, where the woak
  Wer a-spreadèn his head out around,
There the scrags that the wind had a-broke,
20 Wer a-lyèn about on the ground,
Or the childern, wi' little red hands,
Wer a-tyèn em up in their bands;
Vor noo squier or farmer turn'd off
Little childern a-pickèn o' scroff.

There wer woone bloomèn child wi' a cloak
  On her shoulders, as green as the ground;
An' another, as gray as the woak,
  Wi' a bwoy in a brown frock, a-brown'd.
An' woone got up, in plaÿ, vor to taït,
30 On a woak-limb, a-growèn out straïght.
But she soon wer a-taïted down off,
By her meätes out a-pickèn o' scroff.

When they childern do grow to staïd vo'k,
  An' goo out in the worold, all wide
Vrom the copse, an' the zummerleäze woak,
  Where at last all their elders ha' died,
They wull then vind it touchèn to bring,
To their minds, the sweet springs o' their spring,
Back avore the new vo'k did turn off
40 The poor childern a-pickèn o' scroff.

The Rwose in the Dark

In zummer, leäte at evenèn tide,
  I zot to spend a moonless hour
'Ithin the window, wi' the zide
  A-bound wi' rwoses out in flow'r,
Bezide the bow'r, vorsook o' birds,
An' listen'd to my true-love's words.

A-risèn to her comely height,
  She push'd the swingèn ceäsement round;

And I could hear, beyond my zight,
10 The win'-blow'd beech-tree softly sound,
On higher ground, a-swäyèn slow,
On drough my happy hour below.

An' tho' the darkness then did hide
The dewy rwose's blushèn bloom,
He still did cast sweet aïr inside
To Jeäne, a-chattèn in the room;
An' though the gloom did hide her feäce,
Her words did bind me to the pleäce.

An' there, while she, wi' runnèn tongue,
20 Did talk unzeen 'ithin the hall,
I thought her like the rwose that flung
His sweetness vrom his darken'd ball,
'Ithout the wall, an' sweet's the zight
Ov her bright feäce by mornèn light.

The Child an' the Mowers

O, aye! they had woone child bezide,
An' a finer your eyes never met,
'Twer a dear little fellow that died
In the zummer that come wi' such het;
By the mowers, too thoughtless in fun,
He wer then a-zent off vrom our eyes,
Vrom the light ov the dew-dryèn zun, –
Aye! vrom days under blue-hollow'd skies.

He went out to the mowers in meäd,
10 When the zun wer a-rose to his height,
An' the men wer a-swingèn the sneäd,
Wi' their eärms in white sleeves, left an' right;
An' out there, as they rested at noon,
O! they drench'd en vrom eäle-horns too deep,
Till his thoughts wer a-drown'd in a swoon;
Aye! his life wer a-smother'd in sleep.

Then they laid en there-right on the ground,
  On a grass-heap, a-zweltrèn wi' het,
Wi' his heäir all a-wetted around
20 His young feäce, wi' the big drops o' zweat;
In his little left palm he'd a-zet,
  Wi' his right hand, his vore-vinger's tip,
As vor zome'hat he woulden vorget, –
  Aye! zome thought that he woulden let slip.

Then they took en in hwome to his bed,
  An' he rose vrom his pillow noo mwore,
Vor the curls on his sleek little head
  To be blown by the wind out o' door.
Vor he died while the haÿ russled grey
30 On the staddle so leätely begun:
Lik' the mown-grass a-dried by the day, –
  Aye! the zwath-flow'r's a-killed by the zun.

Leaves a-Vallèn

There the ash-tree leaves do vall
  In the wind a-blowèn cwolder,
An' my childern, tall or small,
  Since last Fall be woone year wolder;
Woone year wolder, woone year dearer,
  Till when they do leäve my he'th.
I shall be noo mwore a hearer
  O' their vaïces or their me'th.

There dead ash leaves be a-toss'd
10 In the wind, a-blowèn stronger,
An' our life-time, since we lost
  Souls we lov'd, is woone year longer;
Woone year longer, woone year wider,
  Vrom the friends that death ha' took,
As the hours do teäke the rider
  Vrom the hand that last he shook.

No. If he do ride at night
 Vrom the zide the zun went under,
Woone hour vrom his western light
20 Needen meäke woone hour asunder;
Woone hour onward, woone hour nigher
 To the hopevul eastern skies,
Where his mornèn rim o' vier
 Soon ageän shall meet his eyes.

Leaves be now a-scatter'd round
 In the wind, a-blowèn bleaker,
An' if we do walk the ground
 Wi' our life-strangth woone year weaker;
Woone year weaker, woone year nigher
30 To the pleäce where we shall vind
Woone that's deathless vor the dier,
 Voremost they that dropp'd behind.

Lwonesomeness

As I do zew, wi' nimble hand,
 In here avore the window's light,
How still do all the housegear stand
 Around my lwonesome zight.
How still do all the housegear stand
Since Willie now 've a-left the land.

The rwose-tree's window-sheädèn bow
 Do hang in leaf, an' win'-blow'd flow'rs
Avore my lwonesome eyes do show
10 Theäse bright November hours.
Avore my lwonesome eyes do show
Wi' nwone but I to zee em blow.

The sheädes o' leafy buds, avore
 The peänes, do sheäke upon the glass,
An' stir in light upon the vloor,
 Where now vew veet do pass.

An' stir in light upon the vloor
Where there's a-stirrèn nothèn mwore.

This win' mid dreve upon the maïn,
20 My brother's ship, a-plowèn foam,
But not bring mother, cwold, nor raïn,
At her now happy hwome.
But not bring mother, cwold, nor raïn,
Where she is out o' païn.

Zoo now that I'm a-mwopèn dumb,
A-keepèn father's house, do you
Come of 'en wi' your work vrom hwome,
Vor company. Now do.
Come of 'en wi' your work vrom hwome,
30 Up here a-while. Do come.

The Turnstile

Ah! sad wer we as we did peäce
The wold church road, wi' downcast feäce,
The while the bells, that mwoan'd so deep
Above our child a-left asleep,
Wer now a-zingèn all alive
Wi' tother bells to meäke the vive.
But up at woone pleäce we come by,
'Twer hard to keep woone's two eyes dry;
On Steän-cliff road, 'ithin the drong,
10 Up where, as vo'k do pass along,
The turnèn stile, a-païnted white,
Do sheen by day an' show by night.
Vor always there, as we did goo
To church, thik stile did let us drough,
Wi' spreadèn eärms that wheel'd to guide
Us each in turn to tother zide.
An' vu'st ov all the traïn he took
My wife, wi' winsome gaït an' look;

An' then zent on my little maïd,
A-skippèn onward, overjaÿ'd
To reach ageän the pleäce o' pride,
Her comely mother's left han' zide.
An' then, a-wheelèn roun', he took
On me, 'ithin his third white nook.
An' in the fourth, a-sheäkèn wild,
He zent us on our giddy child.
But eesterday he guided slow
My downcast Jenny, vull o' woe,
An' then my little maïd in black,
A-walkèn softly on her track;
An' after he'd a-turn'd ageän,
To let me goo along the leäne,
He had noo little bwoy to vill
His last white eärms, an' they stood still.

Other Poems in the Dorset Dialect

Which Road?

Still green on the limbs o' the woak wer the leaves,
Where the black slooe did grow, a-meal'd over wi' grey,
Though leäzes, a-burnt, wer wi' bennets a-brown'd,
An' the stubble o' wheat wer a-witherèn white,
While sooner the zunlight did zink vrom the zight,
An' longer did linger the dim-roaded night.

But bright wer the day-light a-dryèn the dew,
As foam wer a-villèn the pool in its vall,
An' a-sheenèn did climb, by the chalk o' the cliff,
10 The white road a-voun' steep to the wayweary step,
Where along by the knap, wi' a high-beätèn breast,
Went the maïd an' the chap to the feäst in their best.

There hosses went by wi' their neck in a bow,
An' did toss up their nose, over outspringèn knees;
An' the ox, heäiryhided, wi' low-swingèn head;
An' the sheep, little knee'd, wi' a quick-dippèn nod;
An' a maïd, wi' her head a-borne on, in a proud
Gaït o' walkèn, so smooth as an aïr-zwimmèn cloud

Jaÿ a-Pass'd

When leaves, in evenèn winds, do vlee,
Where mornèn aïr did strip the tree,
The mind can waït vor boughs in spring
To cool the elem-sheäded ring.
Where orcha'd blooth's white sceäles do vall
Mid come the apple's blushèn ball.

Our hopes be new, as time do goo,
A-measur'd by the zun on high,
Avore our jaÿs do pass us by.

10 When ice did melt below the zun,
An' weäves along the streäm did run,
I hoped in Maÿ's bright froth to roll,
Lik' jess'my in a lily's bowl.
Or, if I lost my loose-bow'd swing,
My wrigglèn kite mid pull my string,
An' when noo ball did rise an' vall,
Zome other geäme wud still be nigh,
Avore my jaÿs all pass'd me by.

I look'd, as childhood pass'd along,
20 To walk, in leäter years, man-strong,
An' look'd ageän, in manhood's pride,
To manhood's sweetest chaïce, a bride:
An' then to childern, that mid come
To meäke my house a dearer hwome.
But now my mind do look behind
Vor jaÿs; an' wonder, wi' a sigh,
When 'twer my jaÿs all pass'd me by.

Wer it when, woonce, I miss'd a call
To rise, an' seem'd to have a vall?
30 Or when my Jeäne to my hands left
Her vew bright keys, a dolevul heft?
Or when avore the door I stood,
To watch a child a-gone vor good?
Or where zome crowd did laugh aloud;
Or when the leaves did spring, or die?
When did my jaÿ all pass me by?

Walkèn Hwome at Night

You then, vor me, meäde up your mind
To leäve your rights o' hwome behind,
Your width o' teäble-rim an' bit
O' virezide vloor, where you did zit,
An' all your walks by stiles and geätes
O' summer vields wi' maïden meätes,
To guide vor me my house, though small,
A-reckon'd, all my house mid be.
Come, hood your head; the wind is keen.
10 Come this zide, here. I'll be your screen.

The clothes your mother put ye on
Be now a-worn all out an' gone,
An' you do wear vrom top to tooe
What my true love ha' bought ye new,
That now in comely sheäpe's a-shown,
My own a-deckèn ov my own;
An' oh! ov all that I've a-got,
Vor your sweet lot a half is small.
Come, hood your head; wrap up, now do.
20 Walk clwose to me. I'll keep ye lew.

An' now when we be out to spend
A vrosty night wi' zome wold friend,
An' ringèn clocks to tell at last
The evenèn hour's a-gone too vast,
Noo vorked roads, to left an' right,
Do sunder us vor night or light;
But all my woe's vor you to veel,
An' all my weal's vor you to know.
Come, hood your head. You can't zee out?
30 I'll leäd ye right, you needèn doubt.

Aïr an' Light

Ah! look an' zee how widely free
To all the land the win' do goo;
If here a tree do swaÿ, a tree
On yon'er hill's a-swaÿen too.
How wide the light do bring to zight
The pleäce an' liven feäce o' man;
How vur the stream do run vor lip
To drink, or hand to sink and dip!

But oone mid be a-smote wi' woe
10 That middèn pass, in wider flight,
To other souls, a-droopèn low,
An' hush'd like birds at vall o' night.
But zome be sad wi' others glad;
In turn we all mid murn our lot,
An' many a day that have a-broke
Oone heart is jaÿ to other vo'k.

The mornèn zun do cast abroad
His light on drops o' dewy wet,
An' down below his noontide road
20 The streams do gleäre below his het;
His evenèn light do sparkle bright
Across the quiv'rèn gossamer;
But I, though fair he still mid glow,
Do miss a zight he cannot show.

The Vierzide Chairs

Though days do gaïn upon the night,
An' birds do teäke a leäter flight,
'Tis cwold enough to spread our hands
Oonce now an' then to glowèn brands.
Zoo now we two, a-left alwone,
Can meäke a quiet hour our own,

Let's teäke, a-zittèn feäce to feäce,
Our pleäces by the vier pleäce,
Where you shall have the window view
10 Outside, an' I can look on you.

When oonce I brought ye hwome my bride,
In yollow glow o' zummer tide,
I wanted you to teäke a chair
At that zide o' the vier, there,
And have the ground an' sky in zight
Wi' feäce toward the window light;
While I back here should have my brow
In sheäde, an' zit where I do now,
That you mid zee the land outside,
20 If I could look on you, my bride.

An' there the water-pool do spread,
Wi' swaÿèn elems over head,
An' there's the knap where we did rove
At dusk, along the high-tree'd grove,
The while the wind did whisper down
Our whisper'd words; an' there's the crown
Ov Duncliffe hill, wi' wid'nèn sheädes
Ov wood a-cast on slopèn gleädes:
Zoo you injoy the green an' blue
30 Without, an' I will look on you.

An' there's the copse, where we did all
Goo out a-nuttèn in the fall,
That now would meäke, a-quiv'rèn black,
But little lewth behind your back;
An' there's the tower, near the door,
That we at dusk did meet avore
As we did gather on the green,
An' you did zee, an' wer a-zeen:
All wold zights welcomer than new,
40 A-look'd on as I look'd on you.

The Stwonen Steps

Theäse stwonen steps a-zet so true
Wi' top on top, a voot each wide,
Did always clim' the slopèn zide
O' theäse steep ledge, vor me an' you.
Had men a-built the steps avore
The mossy arch ov our wold door?
Wer theäse wold steäirs a-laid by man
Avore the bridge's archèd span?
Had vo'k a-put the stwones down here
10 Avore they piled the church's speer?
Ah! who do know how long agoo
The steps vu'st bore a shoe?

An' here bezide the slopèn hump,
Vrom stwone to stwone, a-lyèn flat,
The childern's little veet do pat,
An' men-vo'k's heavy zoles do clump.
Ah! which the last shall beät a shoe
On theäse grey stwones: shall I or you?
Which little boy o' mine shall clim'
20 The steps the last, my John or Jim?
Which maïd, child-quick or woman-slow,
Shall walk the last theäse stwones in row?
Who can ever tell us who
The last shall come or goo?

The road do leäd below the blocks
To yonder springhead's stwonen cove,
An' Squier's house, an elem grove,
An' mill bezide the foamy rocks.
An' aye, theäse well-wore blocks o' stwone
30 Wer here when I vu'st run alwone;
The stwonèn steäirs wer here avore
My father put a voot to vloor.

'Twer up the steps that gramfer come
To court poor grammer at her hwome.
But who can ever tell what peäirs
O' veet trod vu'st the steäirs?

The Vield Path

Here oonce did sound sweet words, a-spoke
In wind that swum
Where ivy clomb,
About the ribby woak;
An' still the words, though now a-gone,
Be dear to me, that linger on.

An' here, as comely vo'k did pass,
Their sheädes did slide
Below their zide,
10 Along the flow'ry grass,
An' though the sheädes be all a-gone,
Still dear's the ground they vell upon.

But could they come where then they stroll'd,
However young
Mid sound their tongue,
Their sheädes would show em wold;
But dear, though they be all a-gone,
Be sheädes o' trees that linger on.

O ashèn poles, a-sheenèn tall!
20 You be too young
To have a-sprung
In days when I wer small;
But you, broad woak, wi' ribby rind,
Wer here so long as I can mind.

The Wind at the Door

As day did darken on the dewless grass,
There still, wi' nwone a-come by me,
To staÿ awhile at hwome by me,
Within the house, all dumb by me,
I zot me sad as evenèntide did pass.

An' there a win'-blast shook the rattlèn door,
An' seem'd, as win' did mwoan without,
As if my Jeäne, alwone without,
A-stannèn on the stwone without,
10 Wer there a-come wi' happiness oonce mwore.

I went to door; an' out vrom trees above
My head, upon the blast by me,
Sweet blossoms wer a-cast by me,
As if my love, a-past by me,
Did fling em down – a token ov her love.

'Sweet blossoms o' the tree where I do murn,'
I thought, 'if you did blow vor her,
Vor apples that should grow vor her,
A-vallèn down below vor her,
20 O then how happy I should zee you kern.'

But no. Too soon I voun' my charm a-broke.
Noo comely soul in white like her –
Noo soul a-steppèn light like her –
An' nwone o' comely height like her –
Went by; but all my grief ageän awoke.

Melhill Feast

Aye there, at the feäst by Melhill's brow,
So softly below the clouds in flight,
Did glide on the wood the sheäde an' light,
Tree after tree, an' bough by bough.

An' there, as among the crowd I took
My wanderèn way, bwoth to an' fro,
Vull comely wer sheäpes the day did show,
Feäce upon feäce, an' look by look.

An' there, among maïdens left an' right,
10 On oone o' the feäirest I did zet
My looks all the mwore the mwore we met,
Glance upon glance, an' zight by zight.

The way she'd a-come by then wer soon
The happiest road that I did goo,
By glitterèn gossamer or dew,
Evenèn by evenèn, moon by moon.

Along by the doors o' maïdens feäir,
As feäir as the best till she is nigh,
Though now I can heedless pass em by,
20 Oone after oone, or peäir by peäir.

Vust by the orcha'ds dim an' cool,
An' then along Woodcombe's timber'd zide,
Then by the meäds, where streäms do glide,
Shallow by shallow, pool by pool.

An' then to the house, a-zet alwone,
Wi' rwoses a-hung on pworch an' wall,
Where up by the bridge the stream do vall,
Rock under rock, an' stwone by stwone.

Sweet wer the hopes that then did cheer
30 My heart as I thought on times to come,
Wi' her vor to bless my happy hwome,
Moon upon moon, an' year by year.

White an' Blue

My love is o' comely height, an' straïght,
An' comely in all her ways an' gaït;
In feäce she do show the rwose's hue,
An' her lids on her eyes be white on blue.

When Elemley clubmen walk'd in Maÿ
An' vo'k come in clusters, ev'ry waÿ,
As soon as the zun dried up the dew,
An' clouds in the sky wer white on blue,

She come by the down, wi' trippèn walk,
10 By deäisies, an' sheenèn banks o' chalk,
An' brooks, where the crowvoot flow'rs did strew
The sky-tinted water, white on blue.

She nodded her head, as plaÿ'd the band;
She dapp'd wi' her voot, as she did stand;
She danced in a reel, a-wearèn new
A skirt wi' a jacket, white wi' blue.

I singled her out vrom thin an' stout,
Vrom slender an' stout I chose her out;
An' what, in the evenèn, could I do,
20 But gi'e her my breast-knot, white an' blue?

The Geäte a-Vallèn to

In the zunsheen ov our zummers
Wi' the haÿ time now a-come,
How busy wer we out a-vield
Wi' vew a-left at hwome,
When waggons rumbled out ov yard
Red wheeled, wi' body blue,
As back behind 'em loudly slamm'd
The geäte a-vallèn to.

Drough daÿsheen ov how many years
10 The geäte ha' now a-swung
Behind the veet o' vull-grown men
An' vootsteps ov the young.
Drough years o' days it swung to us
Behind each little shoe,
As we tripped lightly on avore
The geäte a-vallèn to.

In evenèn time o' starry night
How mother zot at hwome,
An' kept her bleäzèn vire bright
20 Till father should ha' come,
An' how she quicken'd up an' smiled
An' stirred her vire anew,
To hear the trampèn ho'ses' steps
An' geäte a-vallèn to.

There's moon-sheen now in nights o' fall
When leaves be brown vrom green,
When, to the slammèn o' the geäte,
Our Jenny's ears be keen,
When the wold dog do wag his taïl,
30 An' Jeän could tell to who,
As he do come in drough the geäte,
The geäte a-vallèn to.

An' oft do come a saddened hour
When there must goo away
One well-beloved to our heart's core,
Vor long, perhaps vor aye:
An' oh! it is a touchèn thing
The lovèn heart must rue,
To hear behind his last farewell
40 The geäte a-vallèn to.

Poems in National English

(Originally from *Poems Partly of Rural Life in National English*, 1846; *Poems of Rural Life in Common English*, 1868; and manuscript)

Rustic Childhood

No city primness train'd our feet
To strut in childhood through the street,
But freedom let them loose to tread
The yellow cowslip's downcast head;
Or climb, above the twining hop
And ivy, to the elm-tree's top;
Where southern airs of blue-sky'd day
Breath'd o'er the daisy and the may.
  I knew you young, and love you now,
10 O shining grass, and shady bough.

Far off from town, where splendour tries
To draw the looks of gather'd eyes,
And clocks, unheeded, fail to warn
The loud-tongued party of the morn,
We spent in woodland shades our day
In cheerful work or happy play,
And slept at night where rustling leaves
Threw moonlight shadows o'er our eaves.
  I knew you young, and love you now,
20 O shining grass, and shady bough.

Or in the grassy drove by ranks
Of white-stemm'd ashes, or by banks
Of narrow lanes, in-winding round
The hedgy sides of shelving ground;
Where low-shot light struck in to end
Again at some cool-shaded bend,
Where we might see through darkleav'd boughs
The evening light on green hill-brows.
  I knew you young, and love you now,
30 O shining grass, and shady bough.

Or on the hillock where we lay
At rest on some bright holyday;
When short noon-shadows lay below
The thorn in blossom white as snow;
And warm air bent the glist'ning tops
Of bushes in the lowland copse,
Before the blue hills swelling high
And far against the southern sky.
I knew you young, and love you now,
40 O shining grass, and shady bough.

The Eegrass

With stricken heart, and melting mood,
I rov'd along the mead to brood
In freedom, at the eventide,
On souls that time has scatter'd wide;
As by the boughy hedge's side
The shadows darken'd into night,
And cooling airs, with wanton flight,
Were blowing o'er the eegrass.

There fancy roam'd from place to place,
10 From year to year, to find some face
That I no more shall look upon,
Or see in sadness, sorrow-wan,
Or time-worn with its brightness gone;
And my own Lucy, fair to see,
Seem'd there to come again to me,
Up o'er the shining eegrass.

As when upon a summer's day,
While we were there at hawling hay,
With downcast look she lightly drew
20 Her rake-head to her shapely shoe,
With hands well skill'd to bring it through
The tangled crowfoot-stems, that broke
The rakes for us poor clumsy folk,
And still are in the eegrass.

And there the storms that spring clouds shed
Fell lately on her hooded head,
The while she sat, at eventide,
A-milking by her dun cow's side;
And there, when summer, sunny-skied
30 And boughy-wooded, brought its heat,
She trod the flow'rs with light-shod feet,
But comes not o'er the eegrass.

O summer all thy crops are down,
And copse and leaze are turning brown,
And cuckoos leave the boughs to fade
Through waning fall, within the glade;
And we have lost our blooming maid.
So all thou broughtest fresh and fair
Begins to wither ev'ry where,
40 But this bright-bladed eegrass.

Moss

O rain-bred moss that now dost hide
The timber's bark and wet rock's side,
Upshining to the sun, between
The darksome storms, in lively green,
And wash'd by pearly rain drops clean,
Steal o'er my lonely path, and climb
My wall, dear child of silent time.
O winter moss, creep on, creep on,
And warn me of the time that's gone.

10 Green child of winter, born to take
Whate'er the hands of man forsake,
That makest dull, in rainy air,
His labour-brighten'd works; so fair
While newly left in summer's glare;
And stealest o'er the stone that keeps
His name in mem'ry where he sleeps.
O winter moss, creep on, creep on,
And warn us of the time that's gone.

Come lowly plant that lov'st, like me,
20 The shadow of the woodland tree,
And waterfall where echo mocks
The milkmaid's song by dripping rocks,
And sunny turf for roving flocks,
And ribby elms extending wide
Their roots within the hillock's side.
Come winter moss, creep on, creep on,
And warn me of the time that's gone.

Come, meet me wandering, and call
My mind to some green mould'ring hall
30 That once stood high, the fair-wall'd pride
Of hearts that lov'd, and hoped, and died,
Ere thou hadst climb'd around its side:
Where blooming faces once were gay
For eyes no more to know the day.
Come winter moss, creep on, creep on,
And warn me of the time that's gone.

While there in youth, – the sweetest part
Of life, – with joy-believing heart,
They liv'd their own dear days, all fraught
40 With incidents for after-thought
In later life, when fancy brought
The outline of some faded face
Again to its forsaken place.
Come winter moss, creep on, creep on,
And warn me of the time that's gone.

Come where thou climbedst, fresh and free,
The grass-beglooming apple-tree,
That, hardly shaken with my small
Boy's strength, with quiv'ring head, let fall
50 The apples we lik'd most of all,
Or elm I climb'd, with clasping legs,
To reach the crow's high-nested eggs.
Come winter moss, creep on, creep on,
And warn me of the time that's gone.

Or where I found thy yellow bed
Below the hill-borne fir-tree's head,
And heard the whistling east wind blow
Above, while wood-screen'd down below
I rambled in the spring-day's glow,
60 And watch'd the low-ear'd hares upspring
From cover, and the birds take wing.
Come winter moss, creep on, creep on,
And warn me of the time that's gone.

Or where the bluebells bent their tops
In windless shadows of the copse;
Or where the misty west wind blew
O'er primroses that peer'd out through
Thy bankside bed, and scatter'd dew
O'er grey spring grass I watch'd alone
70 Where thou hadst grown o'er some old stone.
Come winter moss, creep on, creep on,
And warn me of the time that's gone.

To a Garden – On Leaving It

Sweet garden! peaceful spot! no more in thee
Shall I e'er while away the sunny hour.
Farewell each blooming shrub, and lofty tree;
Farewell the mossy path and nodding flow'r:
I shall not hear again from yonder bow'r
The song of birds, or humming of the bee,
Nor listen to the waterfall, nor see
The clouds float on behind the lofty tow'r.

No more, at cool-air'd eve, or dewy morn,
10 My gliding scythe shall shear thy mossy green:
My busy hands shall never more adorn,

My eyes no more may see, this peaceful scene.
But still, sweet spot, wherever I may be,
My love-led soul will wander back to thee.

Our Hedges

Aye, which way ran the boughy hedge,
Or north and south, or east and west,
Along the homeground's flow'ry edge
With many a song bird's round-rimm'd nest?
From east to west, in wind that play'd
On one side sunn'd, on one in shade,
   In shade of summer boughs.

Ah! which way ran the flow'ry hedge,
Or north and south, or east and west,
10 Where we in hayfield on the ledge
So often sat for nunch or rest?
From north to south, with one side bright
Till noon, and one from noon to night,
   All bright with summer boughs.

To what blue quarter of the sky
Ran that which we, at times on times,
On Sundays stepp'd so lightly by
Towards the church's loud'ning chimes?
Along its side our path led forth
20 To church uphill, to south from north,
   From north by summer boughs.

And down from church are hedges two
That, side by side, south eastward wend
And skirt the lane that I went through
To see safe home a sweet young friend.
Two happy souls were we between
The hedges two in flow'ry green,
   All green with summer boughs.

Plorata Veris Lachrymis

O now, my true and dearest bride,
Since thou hast left my lonely side,
My life has lost its hope and zest.
The sun rolls on from east to west,
But brings no more that evening rest,
Thy loving-kindness made so sweet,
And time is slow that once was fleet,
    As day by day was waning.

The last sad day that show'd thee lain
10 Before me, smiling in thy pain,
The sun soar'd high along his way
To mark the longest summer day,
And show to me the latest play
Of thy sweet smile, and thence, as all
The daylengths shrunk from small to small,
    My joy began its waning.

And now 'tis keenest pain to see
Whate'er I saw in bliss with thee.
The softest airs that ever blow,
20 The fairest days that ever glow,
Unfelt by thee, but bring me woe.
And sorrowful I kneel in pray'r,
Which thou no longer, now, canst share,
    As day by day is waning.

How can I live my lonesome days?
How can I tread my lonesome ways?
How can I take my lonesome meal?
Or how outlive the grief I feel?
Or how again look on to weal?
30 Or sit, at rest, before the heat
Of winter fires, to miss thy feet,
    When evening light is waning?

Thy voice is still I lov'd to hear,
Thy voice is lost I held so dear.
Since death unlocks thy hand from mine,
No love awaits me such as thine.
Oh! boon the hardest to resign!
But if we meet again at last
In heav'n, I little care how fast
40 My life may now be waning.

My Dearest Wife

Had Mona been, as many are,
Among the stars a shining star,
Another with her beaming face
Might shine upon me in her place.
But no. She shone before my sight
The moon of all my earthly light,
And none like her can ever rise
To lighten my benighted eyes.

The winds o'er bowing saplings fly,
10 The clouds swim on below the sky,
The water winds with ceaseless speed
By woody knowle and grassy mead;
Yet could I ride the water's face,
Or keep the wind's unslackened pace,
Nor stream below nor wind above
Could ever waft me to my love.

But time, that brings the nights and days
With silent flight, that never stays,
And guides the stream from hill to lea
20 To mingle with the rocking sea,
And brings the gathering cloud on high
To waft it from the clearing sky –
Oh! Time alone shall lead me on
At last to where my love is gone.

My Dearest Julia

Oh! can or can I not live on,
Forgetting thee, my love forgone?
'Tis true, where joyful faces crowd
And merry tongues are ringing loud,
Or where some needful work unwrought
May call for all my care and thought,
Or where some landscape, bath'd in light,
May spread to fascinate my sight,
Thy form may melt awhile, as fade
10 Our shades within some welkin shade,
And I awhile may then live on,
Forgetting thee, my love forgone.

But then the thrilling thought comes on,
Of all thy love that's now forgone;
Thy daily toil to earn me wealth,
Thy grief to see me out of health,
Thy yearning readiness to share
The burden of my toil and care,
And all the blessings thou hast wrought
20 In my behalf by deed and thought.
And then I seem to hear thee calling,
Gloomy fac'd with tear drops falling,
'Canst thou then so soon live on,
Forgetful of my love forgone?'

The River Stour

Stour, of all our streams the dearest
Unto me, for thou was nearest
   To my boyhood in my play,
Blest may be the sons and daughters
That beside thy wand'ring waters
   Have their hearth, and spend their day.
By happy homes of high and low
Flow on dark river, ever flow.

Thou through meady Blackmore wendest,
10 And around its hillslopes bendest,
   Under cliffs, and down the dells;
On by uplands under tillage,
On beside the tower'd village,
   With its sweetly-chiming bells.
There go, dear stream, and ever flow
By souls, in joy, without a woe.

Wind around the woody ridges;
Shoot below thy archy bridges,
   Swelling by thy many brooks;
20 Gliding slowly in thy deepness;
Rolling fleetly at thy steepness;
   Whirling round the shady nooks;
And pass the lands that fall and rise
Below the sight of tearless eyes,

Where the willow's head begloometh
Depths below the clote, that bloometh
   Near the rushes' brown-clubb'd wand,
While to mill by mill thou roamest,
And below the mill-weir foamest
30 In the wildly-heaving pond.
And when, at night, the wheel may cease
To roll, may inmates sleep in peace.

Where a hoof or foot onspeedeth
By a well-stein'd road, that leadeth
O'er thy face to either side,
To the town, that's many-streeted,
Where, by loving friends, are greeted
Friend and child, and maid and bride,
May their welfare ne'er give out
40 Until thy stream is dried by drought.

Glowing under day's warm sunning,
Sparkling with thy ripples' running,
Taking to thee brooks and rills,
Valley-draining, dell-bewending,
Water-taking, water-sending,
Down to dairy farms and mills,
O blest below each village tow'r
Be thy by-dwellers, gliding Stour.

The Moor

Where yonder leaning hill-side roves
With woody dippings, far around,
And many jutting brows, and coves,
Of rugged cliffs, and slopy ground,
Beside the stream that slowly sinks
With reaches tinted from the skies,
And stream-side meadows, lowly lies
The moor, with dikes and sedgy brinks.

About us there the willow shade
10 Oft play'd beside the water's edge,
And there the rodded bulrush sway'd
Its soft brown club, above the sedge,
And by the aspen or the bridge,
The angler sat, and lightly whipp'd
His little float, that, dancing, dipp'd
From o'er the waveling's little ridge.

There cows, in clusters, rambled wide,
  Some hanging low their heads to eat,
Some lying on their heavy side,
20 Some standing on their two-peaked feet,
Some sheeted white, some dun or black,
  Some red, and others brindled dark,
  Some marked with milk-white star, or spark,
And ours all white along the back.

There cows, to others, low'd; now here,
  Now there, from open heat to shade;
And out among them, far or near,
  With quiv'ring scream, the horses neigh'd,
The while some boy, within the mead,
30 On some high mare might come astride;
  And sliding down her bulging side,
Might set her, snorting, free to feed.

And there we saw the busy crow
  For mussels down the river play,
And rooks sweep on where men below
  Went, water hemm'd, their crooked way,
And gamb'ling boys, in merry train,
  On holidays came rambling by
  With often-grounded poles, to fly
40 In high-bow'd flight, o'er dike and drain.

There men at work on pathless grass,
  Are seen, though out of hearing, wide,
By neighbour-meeting folk, that pass
  The many-roaded upland side.
So some may like the trampled road,
  O'er well-rubbed stile-bars, with a gloss,
  And some the moor, that some may cross
But pass no door of man's abode.

Lost Shades

How many times the flow'rs have blown
  And died again, from spring to fall,
Since shapes of early friends were shown
  As fair as they among them all.

Or since, below the summer light,
  On banks by daisyheads bespread,
Or fields by yarrow dappled white,
  Their shadows mark'd their comely head.

Or fell at evening on the wall,
10 Beside the door; or glided cool,
By moonpaled timber-stems, to fall
  On glitt'ring dew, or shining pool.

O sun and moon, that love to mark
  All earthborn shapes, or quick, or still,
The wayfarer, the gliding bark,
  The highbough'd tree, or lofty hill;

In your sweet light, so pale or red,
  But sad to me, you seem to miss
The shape of some all-comely head
20 You copied in our day of bliss.

Seasons and Times

Awhile in the dead of the winter,
The wind hurries keen through the sunshine,
But finds no more leaves that may linger
On tree-boughs to strew on the ground.

Long streaks of bright snow-drift, bank-shaded,
Yet lie on the slopes, under hedges;
But still all the road out to Thorndon
Would not wet a shoe on the ground.

The days, though the cold seems to strengthen,
10 Outlengthen their span, and the evening
Seeks later and later its westing,
To cast its dim hue on the ground,

'Till tree-heads shall thicken their shadow
With leaves of a glittering greenness,
And daisies shall fold up their blossoms
At evening, in dew on the ground;

And then, in the plum-warding garden,
Or shadowy orchard, the house-man
Shall smile at his fruit, really blushing,
20 Where sunheat shoots through on the ground.

What season do you feel the fairest –
The season of sowing or growing,
Or season of mowing and ripeness,
When hay may lie new on the ground?

And like you the glittering morning,
Or short-shaded noon, or the coming
Of slant-lighted evening, or moonlight,
When footsteps are few on the ground?

Appendix A:

William Barnes's 'A Dissertation on the Dorset Dialect of the English Language'

1. As increasing communication among the inhabitants of different parts of England, and the spread of school education among the lower ranks of the people, tend to substitute book English for the provincial dialects, it is likely that after a few years many of them will linger only in the more secluded parts of the land, if they live at all; though they would give valuable light to the philologist of that increasing class who wish to purify our tongue and enrich it from its own resources, as well as to the antiquary.

2. The rustic dialect of Dorsetshire, as the author of this dissertation has some reason to think, is, with little variation, that of most of the western parts of England, which were included in the kingdom of the West Saxons, the counties of Surrey, Hants, Berks, Wilts, and Dorset, and parts of Somerset and Devon, and has come down by independent descent from the Saxon dialect which our forefathers, the followers of Cerdic and Cynric, Porta, Stuf, and Wihtgar, brought from the south of Denmark; their inland seat, which King Alfred calls 'Eald Saexen' or Old Saxony, in what is now Holstein, and the three islands Nordstrand, Busen, and Heiligoeland: (see Turner's *History of the Anglo-Saxons*) as the dialects of some of the eastern, middle, and northern counties – which formerly constituted the kingdoms of the East and Middle Angles, the Mercians, the Northumbrians, the Deiri, and Bernicians – might have been derived immediately from that of the founders of those kingdoms, the Angles, who came from 'Anglen' or Old England, in what is now the duchy of Slesvig: and it is not only credible, but most likely, that the Saxons of Holstein and the Angles of Slesvig, might speak different dialects of the common Teutonic tongue even in Denmark.

The modern Danish and Swedish are so much like English that some sentences of those languages, as uttered by a Dane or

Swede, would be intelligible to an Englishman who might not have learnt them. Such as in Danish: –

'*Hans mad var graæshopper og vild honning.*' (Matthew iii. 4)

'His meat was locusts and wild honey.'

'*Han sagde til dem, folger efter mig.*' (Matthew iv. 19)

'He said to them follow after me.'

And in Swedish: –

'*Kom låt oss jå.*'

'Come let us go.'

'*Vi ha god vind.*'

'We have a good wind.'

'*Hvad skepp är det vi se?*' (*Skepp* being pronounced *shepp*.)

'What ship is that we see?' (Wåhlin's *Swedish Grammar*)

3. From the history of the foundation of the kingdom of the West Saxons, which we have in the *Saxon Chronicle* and other ancient authorities, one would infer that the county of Dorset was one of the last of their acquisitions from the British power; though it is not easy to decide whether the Saxon writers have omitted some battle by which they became masters of Dorchester – at that time called Durnovaria, and an important city of the Durotriges, a tribe of Romanized Britons, whose original hill city was Maiden Castle, near Dorchester – or whether its inhabitants submitted to the Saxon power at the overthrow of some of the more easterly Britons in Wiltshire or Hampshire.

4. The founder of the West Saxon kingdom was Cerdic, who landed, in 495, with his son Cynric, and five ships, which, after the rational computation of Turner, would carry five or six hundred men, at Cerdices Ora, as it was subsequently called, a spot which must be somewhere on the coast of Hampshire, though Turner says, 'a remarkable passage in the *Saxon Chronicle*, which indicates that he attacked "West Saexnaland" six years after his arrival (501) induces a belief that his first attempt was on some other part of the island.' So Ethelwerd tells us (834) that 'Sexto etiam anno adventûs eorum occidentalem circumiêrunt Britanniæ partem quæ Westsexe nuncupatur,' though *circumiêrunt*, 'they went round', the verb used by Ethelwerd, may mean only that they sailed round the West of England without landing. In the same year (501) the crews of two Saxon ships with two or three hundred men under Porta, landed and defeated the Britons

at Portsmouth, which was called after him Porta's mouth or Porta's haven; and thirteen years afterwards (in 514) other Saxons were brought to England by Cerdic's nephews, Stuf and Wihtgar.

5. Cerdic and Cynric could not have extended their power much beyond that part of Hampshire where they landed for many years; for in 508, thirteen years after their coming, they had to maintain their footing in a battle with a British King, Natanleod, who resisted them with 5,000 men, with whom he fell at a place which the Saxons afterwards called 'Natan leaga', or Natan's field, now corrupted into Netley, near Southampton; and Porta was met by a British force at Portsmouth, as Stuf and Wihtgar were in 514 at Cerdices Ora, Cerdic's first landing place: and it is not till the year 519, twenty-four years after their coming, when they beat the Britons at Cerdicsford or Charford, that they are said to have founded a kingdom at all; as the *Saxon Chronicle* tells us that then Cerdic and Cynric 'West Saexna rice onfengun', began the West Saxon kingdom. And as they had another battle with the Britons at Cerdices-leah in 528, and in 530 took the Isle of Wight with great slaughter, we must infer that at Cerdic's death, in 534, Dorsetshire, with its important city of Romanized Britons, Durnovaria or Dorchester, was still in the hands of the Britons, whose language was the only one spoken in the neighbourhood.

6. In 552 Cynric defeated the Britons at 'Searobyrig', Salisbury, and four years afterwards at 'Beranbirig', considered to be Banbury in Oxfordshire; and unless the inhabitants of Durnovaria (Dorchester), fell – as they most likely did – in union with those of Sorbiodunum or Salisbury, or in some unrecorded battle of that time, they were free at the death of Cynric.

7. We cannot learn that his successor Caelwin, third king of Wessex, came to Durnovaria, though he made great inroads upon the Britons in other directions; his brother having beaten them at Bedford, and taken four of their towns, Lygeanburh, Æglesburh, Bennington, and Egonesham, supposed by Gibson to be Leighton in Bedfordshire, Aylesbury in Buckinghamshire, and Bensington and Ensham in Oxfordshire, and he himself, six years afterwards, having overcome and slain three British kings, Conmail, Condidan, and Farinmail, at Deorham, now Durham; and after the battle three of the great cities of the Britons, Gloucester,

Cirencester, and Bath, submitted to him, though Durnovaria seems to have been left unaffected by this war. Seven years afterwards, however, the Britons met him at Fetanleagh, and, after a hard battle, in which his son was slain, and he, after being nearly beaten, won the day, he 'gehwearf thonan to his agenum,' returned to his own kingdom, as the *Saxon Chronicle* tells us, a proof that the part of England where he had fought was not his own.

8. But the British neighbours of the West Saxons were so far from being extirpated or perfectly overthrown, that in 659, when Cenwalh was implicated in hostilities with Penda, king of the Mercians, for having repudiated Penda's sister, his queen, the Britons invaded his dominions, and he beat them at Penn-hill, near Crewkerne, and drove them to the Parret, which rises at Cheddington and runs down about four miles west of Penn-hill. Turner infers that the hostile Britons defeated at Penn-hill had come in from the British states of Devon and Cornwall, and it is not unlikely that the Durotriges of Durnovaria, about sixteen miles distant, were among them.

9. The *Saxon Chronicle*, of the battle of King Kenwalh with the Britons at Penn in the year 658, allows us to believe that the river Parret was for a long time the understood line of separation between the kingdom of the West Saxons and the land still held by the Western Britons, as it tells us that in the year 658 'Cenwalh gefeaht æt Peonnum with Wealas, and hy geflymde oth Pedridan.' Kenwalh fought at Penn with the Welsh (Britons) and pursued them to the Parret. Sir R. C. Hoare and others have placed this battle at Penn Zellwood, near Mere, in Wiltshire; making the Saxons to have followed the Britons through bogs, woods, and streams, between twenty and thirty miles: but those who know the neighbourhood of Crewkerne, in Somersetshire, would rather believe that, if Kenwalh chased the Britons from any place which still bears the name of Penn, it was Penn-Hill or Pen Domer, four or five miles east of the river Parret, which runs down between it and Crewkerne: and as we cannot well conceive why the Saxons should stop at the Parret unless it had been an insuperable obstacle, or an understood limit of their dominion, and as we know it could be no greater obstacle to them than to their enemies, we can only take the other conclusion that the land beyond it was at that time held by the Britons. This opinion is

allowed by a fact which is stated by Mr Jennings, who, in his observations on some of the dialects of the West of England, says that 'the district which his glossary is designed to include, embraces the whole of the county of Somerset east of the river Parret, as well indeed as part of Wiltshire and Gloucestershire; many of the words being common to all these counties. In the district west of the river Parret, the pronunciation and many of the words were very different indeed, so as to designate strongly the people who use them,' and, after giving some examples of verbs and pronouns from the dialect west of the Parret, he tells us that 'it pervades, not only the more western parts of Somersetshire, but also the whole of Devonshire.' This assertion is corroborated by Mr Petheram, the author of *An Historical Sketch of the Progress and Present State of Anglo-Saxon Literature in England*, who says, in a very kind and valuable letter to the author of these Poems, 'It must have been often remarked by those conversant with the dialects of Somerset, east and west of the Parret, that the latter approximates to the Devon variety, whilst to the eastward it comes nearer to that of Dorset and Wilts. I do not think it easy to find any where so great a dissimilarity in places so near to each other as is to be met with in this instance. The fact is so, but I am unable to account for it.' The fact is accounted for by the *Saxon Chronicle* if it justifies the author's opinion of the early western limit of the Saxon dominions; though it may not be easy to learn whether the western parts of Somerset and Devonshire were afterwards taken by Saxons who were not of the original Hampshire stock of West Saxons, or by mingled settlers from different Anglo-Saxon kingdoms; or whether the Saxons went west of the Parret, and the dialect of West Saxony was afterwards corrupted in Dorset, Wilts, and Hampshire by Saxons from other parts of England after the union of the heptarchy under Egbert. Athelstan seems to have first extended the Saxon rule to Exeter, which he is said to have separated from the British kingdom of Cornwall.

10. From all these circumstances, therefore, it seems likely that Dorsetshire fell under the power of the West Saxons, and received their language, the venerable parent of its present rustic dialect, with Salisbury, in 552; though the Britons were not driven far beyond the Parret till after the time of Cenwalh, one hundred years later, as Mr Boswell, in his *Diocese of Bristol*, offers reasons

for believing that St Birin, who baptized King Cynegils in 634, was bishop of Dorchester, in Dorsetshire. We know Egbert to have held Dorset in 832, as he was defeated by the Danes off Charmouth. In 876 the Danes took the castle of Wareham, and invaded Dorsetshire from the mouth of the Frome in 998; and in 934 a Bishop of Sherborne took soldiers to Athelstan's camp. Having said so much of the kingdom of the West Saxons, from whose language the Dorset dialect is directly derived, the author will go on to make a few observations on its structure and features.

11. The Dorset dialect is a broad and bold shape of the English language, as the Doric was of the Greek. It is rich in humour, strong in raillery and hyperbole, and altogether as fit a vehicle of rustic feeling and thought, as the Doric is found in the Idyllia of Theocritus.

Some people, who may have been taught to consider it as having originated from corruption of the written English, may not be prepared to hear that it is not only a separate offspring from the Anglo-Saxon tongue, but purer and more regular than the dialect which is chosen as the national speech; purer, inasmuch as it uses many words of Saxon origin for which the English substitutes others of Latin, Greek, or French derivation; and more regular, inasmuch as it inflects regularly many words which in the national language are irregular.

12. In English, purity is in many cases given up for the sake of what is considered to be elegance. Instead of the expression of the common people 'I will not be put upon,' we are apt to consider it better language to say 'I will not be imposed upon,' though the word *imposed* is the Latin *impositum*, put upon; from *in*, upon, and *pono*, to put. For 'I cannot make it out,' again we say 'I cannot effect it,' though *effect* is from the Latin *effectum*, the supine of *efficio*, to make out, from *ex*, out, and *facio*, to make; and for 'I stand to it,' we take 'I insist on it,' though to insist is the Latin *sisto*, to stand, and *in*, upon: so that in these and other such cases we use in what we consider the better expression, the very same words as in the worse; or we take, instead of two English words, a Latin compound, which, from the laws upon which languages are constructed, and the limited range of choice which the human mind has in constructing expressions for the same idea, is made of the very simples which we reject.

13. We shall see this more fully in comparing a few more English expressions in which Latin words are used, with like expressions in the Dorset dialect, the pure, but rejected Saxon words of which are compounded of the same simples as the Latin ones substituted for them: –

'I looked out var ye.'

'I expected you.' *Expected* being a compound from *ex*, out, and *specto*, to look.

'I zeed the upshut ō't.'

'I saw the conclusion of it.' *Conclusion* being made from *con cludo*, to shut up.

'Why b' ye a-cast down?'

'Why are you dejected?' *Dejected* being formed from *de-jacto*, to cast down.

'I don't wish to run into debt.'

'I do not wish to incur debts.' *Incur* being formed of *in*, into, and *curro*, to run.

'I zet myzelf agien it.'

'I opposed it.' *Opposed* being compounded of *ob*, against, and *pono*, to set.

''Twer put out var ziale.'

'It was exposed for sale.' *Exposed* being made from *ex*, out, and *pono*, to put.

'I'll stan' by what ya da zæ.'

'I will stand by your decision.' An idea for which the Romans used a like expression. 'Si quis,' says Cæsar, speaking of the Druids, 'eorum decreto non steterit sacrificiis interdicunt.' If any one may not have stood by their decree, they forbid him the sacrifices.

'He vell in wi' his opinion.'

'He coincided with his opinion.' *Coincide* being derived from *incido*, to fall in, *co*, with.

To esteem a thing of no value or importance is sometimes in Dorset, 'to tiake it var nothen,' as in the Latin, 'Ducegat pro nihilo pecuniam Anacharsis.' Anacharsis took money for nothing, or considered money of no value.

'The common is a-took in.'

'The common is inclosed.' *Inclosed* being from the compound *in-cludo*, to shut in.

A speaker of the Dorset dialect would most likely call balancing or settling an account, 'putten ō't stràight,' putting it straight; an expression which, however vulgar it may sound, is authorized by the Greek language; since, to quote a note of Valpy's Prometheus of Æschylus on the word ὑπεύθυνος, 'at Athens public officers, before they quitted office, sent in their accounts εὔθυναι, to be audited by persons called εὐθύνται (straighteners) from εὐθύνειν, to make straight.'

14. In hundreds of cases such as those which have been given, the elegance of the Latin compound words used instead of the English simple ones, must be only in their sound or the union of the prepositions or adverbs with the verbs from which they are formed. Many of them, however, have no better sound than the English ones of which they take place; and, if the separation of the preposition from its verb excludes elegance it is frequently wanting in Homeric Greek, as well as in German.

The dialectic or English adverbs, well studied, would illustrate the compound verbs of other languages, such as Latin and Greek.

Up, for example, as used adverbially, has three meanings, resolvable, however, into one: –

1st – Up, the opposite of down, as 'Tiake up the book.'

2nd – Up, into a right or good state, from a wrong or bad state, as 'Zweep up the house,' 'Wash up the linen,' 'Rub up the vire-irons.'

3rd – Up, altogether, as 'Zweep the carn up in the carner.' A sense in which it coincides with the Latin *co*, *con*, *com*, as

co-emo	to buy up	con-cipio	to catch up
col-ligo	to gather up	con-cludo	to shut up
col-loco	to pliace or put up	con-gero	to drow up
com-buro	to burn up	con-jugo	to yoke up
com-edo	to eat up	con-sarcio	to zew or mend up
com-misceo	to mix up	con-seco	to cut up
com-plico	to vuold up	con sequor	to vollee up
com-pono	to put up (medicine)	con-signo	to seal up
com-primo	to squeeze up	con-tineo	to hold up

The prepositional affix, *co*, *con*, *com*, is often neglected by Latin readers, who make no difference between such words as *signo* and *consigno*, *edo* and *comedo*; though to eat one's bread is not always to eat *up* one's bread; and to seal a conveyance is not always to seal it *up*.

15. The following and other verbs are regular in the Dorset dialect though irregular in national English: –

	English past tense	*Dorset past tense*
blow	blew	blowed
build	built	builded
burst	burst	busted
catch	caught	catched
crow	crew	crowed
draw	drew	drā'd
gild	gilt	gilded
grow	grew	growed
hide	hid	hided
know	knew	knowed
run	ran	runned or rinned
slide	slid	slided
throw	threw	drowed

16. The Dorset dialect, like others, differs from the national speech by substitutions, which are far from being irregular, of one articulation or pure sound for another.

The pure sounds of the English language for some of which the Dorset dialect substitutes others, are sixteen long and short: four long and four short close ones, and four long and four short open ones.

Close sounds	*Long*	*Short*
	1st, ee in meet	1st, i in wit
	2nd, e long in the western dialects	2nd, i in dip
		3rd, e in men
		4th, e in battery or e of the French article *le*
	3rd, a in mate	
	4th, ea in earth	

Open sounds	*Long*	*Short*
	1st, a in father	1st, a in fat
	2nd, aw in awe	2nd, o in dot
	3rd, o in rope	3rd, u in lull
	4th, oo in food	4th, oo in crook

17. Table of cognate letters or kinsletters for the changes of the consonants.

Some of the letters of the lips, teeth, palate, and throat, are fellows by two and two, or kinsletters; each of a pair spelling the same articulation as the other, but with a stronger or weaker, or a rougher or smoother expulsion of the breath: and the Dorset dialect in many cases substitutes the smoother of two kinsletters for the rougher one of the English language.

	Rough	*Smooth*
Lip kinsletters	p in pin	b in bin
Teeth kinsletters	th in thin	th in thee
	f in	v in vine
Close palate kinsletters	t in tie	d in die
Open palate kinsletters	s in sun	z in zone
	ch in chin	j in jin
Throat kinsletters	k in kill	g in gill
	c in cap	g in gap

18. In the Dorset dialect *a* is frequently substituted for *e*: as in *bag*, beg; *bagger*, begger; *kag*, keg; *agg*, egg; *lag*, leg.

19. For the first long close sound of *ea*, as in *beaver*, *dream*, the second is often substituted, as *bœver*, *dræm*, or the diphthong *ee*, *a* of the first close and first open sound, as *leäd*, lead, *cleän*, clean. *'e* for the pronoun *he* unemphatical is the fourth short close sound of *e* in battery, or like the *e* of the French pronoun *le*.

20. The sound of the vowel *e* long is the second long close one, an intermediate one between that of the English *a* in male, and *ee* in meet; or the tongue, in pronouncing it, approaches the palate nearer than in sounding *a* but not so near as in sounding *ee*. The author has written it *æ* or *ë*.

21. The Dorset dialect, in most cases, substitutes the diphthongal sound *iā* or *yā*, the first close and first open sound, for the English third long close sound *a* as that in bake, cake, hate, late, mate; making those words *biake*, *kiake*, *hiate*, *liate*, *miate*; the very change which the Spanish language has made in the same sound – that of *e*, in many Italian words; such as *bene*, *certo*, *inverno*, *serra*, *tempo*, *vento*, which are in Spanish *bien*, *cierto*, *invierno*, *sierra*, *tiempo*, *viento*.

22. The diphthongs *ai* or *ay* and *ei* or *ey*, the third long close sound as in *May*, *hay*, *maid*, *paid*, *vein*, *neighbour*, *prey*, are sounded – like the Greek *ai* – the *a* or *e* the first open sound as *a* in father and the *i* or *y* as *ee* the first close sound. The author has marked the *a* of diphthongs so sounded with a circumflex; as *Mây*, *hây*, *mâid*, *pâid*, *vâin*, *nêighbour*, *prây*.

23. The third close sound of *a* in mate is often substituted in Dorset for the first open one of *a* in rather; as *fāther*, father; *lāfe*, laugh; *ā'ter*, after; *hāfe*, half. The author has in this case marked it *ā*. The diphthong *i* in *chime* and *shine* becomes *ee* making those words *cheem* and *sheen*.

24. The second long open sound, as of *a* in fall and of *aw* in jaw, is sometimes turned into the third close one *ā*, as *vāl*, in some parts *val*, fall; *jā*, jaw; *strā*, straw: though *brought* becomes *brote*, and fought becomes diphthongal, *foüght*, of the third and fourth open sounds.

25. The second long open sound of *o* in such words as corn, for, horn, morning, storm, becomes the first long open one, *a*, making *carn*, *var*, *harn*, *marnen*, *starm*.

26. The diphthong *oi*, as Mr Jennings observes of the Somerset dialect, is commonly changed for *wī*, as spwile for spoil; *bwile* for boil; *pwīnt* for point; *pwison* for poison; and so on.

27. The third long sound of *o* and *oa* of English words such as bold, cold, fold, more, oak, rope, boat, coat, becomes the diphthong *uo* of the fourth and third short open sounds in the Dorset dialect, in which those words are *buold*, *cuold*, *vuold*, *muore*, *woak*, *ruope*, *büot*, *cüot*; a change of which we find examples in Italian, in such words as *buono*, *cuore*, *luogo*, *uomo*, from the Latin *bonus*, *cor*, *locus*, *homo*; and in parallel changes which the Spanish language makes of the Italian *o* into *ue*; as in *buena*, *cuerpo*, *fuerza*, *nuevo*, *puente*; which are the Italian words *bona*, *corpo*, *forza*, *novo*, *ponte*. *ow* at the end of a word as fellow, hollow, mellow, pillow, yellow, mostly become *er*, making those words *feller*, *holler*, *meller*, *piller*, *yoller*.

28. The first short close sound of *i* in such words as bridge, ridge, will, becomes the third open one of *u*, making *brudge*, *rudge*, *wull*.

So *wolle* and *woll* for *will* is found in the *Harrowing of Hell*, a miracle play of the time of Edward II.

'With resoun wolle ich haven hym.'
'With reason will I have them.'
'Ressoun wol y telle the.'
'I will tell thee a reason.'

29. *d* is substituted for initial *th*; as *drow* for throw; *droo*, through; *drash*, thrash; *drong*, throng; *droat*, throat; *drashel*, threshold.

30. *d*, after *n*, as in *an'*, and; *boun'*, bound; *groun'*, ground; *roun'*, round; *soun'*, sound; is commonly thrown out, as it is after *l*; as in *veel*, for field.

31. *f* of English words is commonly rejected for its smooth kinsletter *v* before a vowel or liquid in the Dorset dialect, in which fast, fetch, feed, find, fire, for, foot, from, become *vast*, *vetch*, *veed*, *vind*, *vire*, *var*, *voot*, *vrom* (see Article 16), and in the Swedish language *f* is pronounced as *v* at the end of a word.

'*Gif lif at den bild*' –'Give life to the image' being pronounced '*Giv liv at den bild.*'

But some English words beginning with *f* before a consonant, as fling, friend, retain *f*. The preposition *of* loses its *f* and becomes *o'* before a consonant. *f* sometimes gave place to its smooth kinsletter *v* in old English.

'The voxe hird' for 'The fox heard' is found in a song of the fourteenth century, in which we find also 'In pes withoute vyhte' for 'In peace without fight.'

32. The liquids *lm* at the end of a word are sometimes parted by a vowel, as in *elem*, elm; *auverwhelem*, overwhelm; *helem*, helm.

33. The liquids *rl* of English words, such as purl, twirl, world, have frequently *d* inserted between them, making *purdle*, *twirdle*, *wordle*. In this case the dialect adopts a principle of articulation of the Greek language, which inserts *d* between the liquids *νρ* in *αν-δ-ρος* for *ανρος* the genitive case of *ανηρ*, a man.

34. *r* in great, pretty, undergoes metathesis, making *ghirt* and *pirty*.

35. *r* before a hissing palate letter, *s*, *c*, or *z*, or *th*, as in burst, first, verse, force, furze, nurs'd, mirth, earth, birth, worth, is thrown out, making *bust*, *vust*, *vess*, *fuoss*, *vuzz*, *nuss'd*, *meth*, *eth*, *beth*, *woth*.

36. *s* before a vowel often but not universally becomes in Dorset its smooth kinsletter *z*, making sand, *zand*; sap, *zeap*;

send, *zend*; set, *zet*; sick, *zick*; some, *zome*; sop, *zop*; and sun, *zun*.

37. In many English words ending with *s* and a mute consonant, those letters have undergone metathesis, since in Anglo-Saxon the *s* followed the consonant, as it does in the Dorset dialect; in which clasp is *claps*; crisp, *crips*; hasp, *haps*; wasp, *waps*; and to ask, to *aks* (*ax*), the Anglo-Saxon *axian*.

38. Where the English rough articulation *th*, as in *thin*, the Anglo-Saxon *þ*, becomes in Dorsetshire its soft kinsletter *th* as in *thee*, the Anglo-Saxon *ð*, as it does very frequently, the author has printed it in italics *th*, as *th*ink.

39. An open palate letter is sometimes substituted for a close one, *r* for *d*; or *k* for *t*; as *parrick*, a paddock; *pank*, to pant.

40. *v* is sometimes omitted, as *gi'e*, give; *ha'*, have; *sar*, serve.

41. The Dorset dialect retains more abstract nouns than the national speech of the pattern of *growth* and *dearth*, formed from verbs and adjectives by shortening their long vowels and affixing *th* or *t* to them: as *blowth* or *blooth*, from *blow*; the blossom of trees; *drîth*, dryness or drought, from *dry*; *lewth*, shelter, from *lew*; *heft*, weight, from the verb *to heave*.

42. The termination *ing* of verbal nouns such as *singing* and *washing*, as well as imperfect participles, is in Dorset *en*; as in a *beäten*, a beating; *writen*, writing.

43. The masculine pronoun *he* or *'e* is still used in Dorset for inanimate nouns, as *he* was in Anglo-Saxon; in which language, as a consequence of its case-endings, many things without life were taken as of the masculine or feminine gender. Indeed it is sometimes said in joke that every thing is *he* but a tom cat, and that is *she*.

44. Many nouns have in the Dorset dialect the old plural termination *en* instead of *s*: as *cheesen*, cheeses; *housen*, houses; *vuzzen*, (*furzen*) furzes; *chicken*, chicks. It is a common blunder, however grammatical it may be thought, to say a *chicken* for a chick; and *chickens* for chicken. We may as well say an *oxen*, and two *oxens*.

45. The possessive case is in Dorset often given with the preposition *of*, *o'*; instead of the case-ending *s*; as 'the tàil ō't' for 'its tâil'; though there is some little difference between one construction and the other; for 'Look at the lags ō'n' would

commonly intimate to a second person that they were something to laugh at, whereas if they were something to excite admiration or compassion, being broken or wounded for example, we should most likely say, 'Look at his lags.'

46. The accusative case of *he* is *en* not *him*, the Anglo-Saxon *hine*. 'He arærde hine up,' 'He raised him up;' and the accusative case of they is *em*, the Anglo-Saxon *hym* or *him*. 'Fæder forgyf *him*,' 'Father, forgive them.' Luke xxiii. 34)

We find *hem* for *them* in Sir John Maundervile's *Travels*, written in the early part of the fourteenth century. In speaking of the antipodes he says, 'it semethe *hem* that wee ben under *hem*.' In Dorset, 'da seem to em that we be under em.'

When a pronoun in an oblique case is emphatical it is given in its nominative shape instead of its objective case. We should say unemphatically, 'Gi'e me the pick;' or 'Gi'e en the knife;' or 'Gi'e us the whēat;' or 'Gi'e em ther money;' but emphatically 'Gi'e the money to *I*, not *he*;' or 'to *we*', not 'to *they*'. This is an analagous substitution to that of the emphatical dative case for the nominative case in French, as 'Je n' irais pas, *moi*.' '*I* shall not go.'

47. The demonstrative pronouns *theos* or *theeas*, is the Anglo-Saxon *þeos*; and *thik*, the Anglo-Saxon *Se ylc*, or the Scotch *the ilk*, the same.

Theos and *thik* are, however, applied only to individual nouns, and not to quantities of matter, which in Anglo-Saxon were of the neuter gender, and which we should still name as *this* or *that*. We may say *theos* or *thik* tree, or stuone, but it would be wrong to say *theos* or *thik* water or milk. It would be *this* or *that* water or milk.

Who and *which* are in Dorset as well as in Anglo-Saxon used only as interrogative pronouns. The relative pronoun is *that*, the Anglo-Saxon *þæt*.

48. The Dorset dialect retains more than the English of the adjectives ending in *en*, meaning made of the noun to which the *en* is put on; as *leatheren*, made of leather; *harnen*, made of horn; *piaperen*, made of paper; *hempen*, made of hemp; *ashen*, *elemen*, *woaken*; made of ash, elm, or oak.

This termination should be retained in English for the sake of distinction, for a paper bag is rightly a bag to put paper in, as a wood house is a house to put wood in: a bag made of paper is a *piaperen* bag, not a paper bag; and a house built of wood is a *wooden* house, not a wood house.

49. The verb *to be* is in the Dorset dialect and Anglo-Saxon:

Dorset	*A. Saxon*	*Dorset*	*A. Saxon*
I be	Ic beo	We be	We beoð
Thee bist	Ðu byst	You be	Ge beoð
He is	He is	Thē be	Hi beoð
And			
I wer	Ic wære	We wer	We wæron
Thee werst	Ðu wære	You wer	Ge wæron
He wer	He wære	Thē wer	Hi wæron

50. The auxiliary verb *may* and *might* is in Dorset *mid*.

51. In negative expressions, the word *not*, after an auxiliary verb ending in *d* or *s*, becomes *en* or *n*; as I *cooden*, I could not; I *shoodden*, I should not; I *woodden*, I would not; I *didden*, I *midden*, I *mossen*, I did not, I may not, I must not.

52. Jennings in his observations on the Western dialects says, 'Another peculiarity is that of attaching to many of the common verbs in the infinitive mode, as well as to some other parts of different conjugations the letter *y*. Thus it is very common to say, *I can't sewy*, *I can't nursy*, *he can't reapy*, *he can't sawy*; as well as *to sewy*, *to nursy*, *to reapy*, *to sawy*, etc., but never, I think, without an auxiliary verb, or the sign of the infinitive *to*.' The truth is that in the author's mother dialect the verb takes *y* only when it is absolute, and never with an accusative case. We may say *Can ye zewy?* but never *Wull ye zewy up theos zēam? Wull ye zew up theos zēam?* would be good Dorset.

53. A verb is commonly conjugated in the present tense with the auxiliary verb *do*, *da*.

I da work	We da work
Thee dast work	You da work
He da work	Thē da work

and in the imperfect tense with *did*; as

I did work
Thee didst work, etc.

The pronoun *it* is commonly omitted before the auxiliary verb *da*: as *da râin*, it rains; *da grow*, it grows; *da seem*, it seems.

54. The verb, however, is generally conjugated with *did* only in the imperfect tense properly so called; or in the case in which it means a continuation or repetition of the action, like the Greek or French imperfect tense as it differs from the aorist or preterite; as 'The vo'ke *did die* by scores;' 'The people kept dying or were dying by scores;' while the semelfactive or single action is named by the simple shape of the verb without the auxiliary *did*; being equal to the Greek aorist or French preterite; as ''E *died* eester-dae.' 'He died yesterday.' This difference of the iterative and semelfactive or aoristic action, which is marked by a different shape of the verb in Greek, Latin, Russian, Persian, French, Italian and other languages, is lost from the English verb with the use of *did*, and in this case the Dorset dialect has an advantage over the national speech.

55. The Dorset dialect is remarkable as retaining in the perfect participle of verbs a *syllabic augment* which is found in Anglo-Saxon and German, though the English language has lost it. In German this augment is *ge*, as

GE-*hangen*, hung; from *hangen*, to hang
GE-*sungen*, sung; from *singen*, to sing
GE-*sehen*, seen; from *sehen*, to see

In Anglo-Saxon it is *ge* or *a*, the latter of which is that retained in Dorsetshire, as

'He've A*lost* his hatchet.'
'She've A*broke* the dish.'

Anglo-Saxon: 'Paulus GE*bunden* wearth GE*send* to Rome.' – *Saxon Chronicle*, AD 50.

Dorset: 'Paul A*bound* wer A*zent* to Rome.'

Anglo-Saxon: 'Simon se apostle wæs A*hangen*.' – *Saxon Chronicle*, AD 90.

Dorset: 'Simon th' apostle wer A*hanged*.'

Anglo-Saxon: 'Feole dwild wearen GE*seogen* and GE*heord*.'

Dorset: 'Many ghosts wer A-*zeed* an' A*hierd*.'

The augment *ge* or *a* of the Anglo-Saxon became *y* or *i* in its transition into the English, as in Y*clep'd*, called; from the Anglo-Saxon *clypian*, to call; a word used by Milton.

> Come thou Goddess fair and free
> In Heav'n Y*clep'd* Euphrosyne. – *L'Allegro*

In the works of Spenser we find the augment *y* in common use.

> She was Y*elod*
> All in silken camus, lily white. – Spenser

Perhaps the only example of the augmented participle in modern English is the word A*shamed*, from the verb *to shame*.

56. Our useful adjectives ending in *some*, as *quarrelsome*, *delightsome*, equivalent to the Latin ones in *us*, *bundus*, *ulentus* and *torius*; naming the state of a noun apt or given to do an action, would have been well taken from any dialect in which they might be found into the national speech, instead of those borrowed from the Latin: as *heedsome*, *attentive*.

57. In the use of the verbs *to go*, and *to do*, to quote a remark of Mr Petherham on the Somerset dialect, and equally true of that of Dorset, we hear frequently such combinations as the following from apocope of the vowel *o*: g'out (go out); *g'in* (go in); *g'auver* (go over); *g'under* (go under); *g'up* (go up); *d'off* (do off); *d'on* (do on); *d'out* (do or put out).

58. Some words of provincial use belong to a class the formation of which, though worthy of attention, has been overlooked by most if not all English grammarians.

From verbs, by the addition of the ending *l*, or *l* with a vowel before or after it, have been formed the names of things by or to which the actions are done, as

Beodan, past tense *bead*, to tell or command, to bid	A. S. bydel, a beadle	one who bids in the name of a magistrate. 'And se bydel þe sende on cwertern,' – Luke xiii. 58
bind, or A. S. bund	bundle	what is bound
bow, to bend	bowl?	what has its surface everywhere bending equally
creep	cripple (creeple)	one who creeps
A. S. fleon, to fly	*flegel*, a flail	what flies around
gird	girdle	what girds

A. S. grafan, to dig	gravel	what is dug, in distinction from rock which cannot be dug
hand	handle	what is taken by the hand
lade, to dip up	ladle	what dips up
nip, to bite	nipple	what is bitten by a child
nod	noddle	what nods; the head
prick	prickle	what pricks
A. S. arædan, to read or guess	riddle	a question to which an answer is to be guessed
rub	Dorset, rubble	what is rubbed into small parts
A. S. scufan, to thrust, push	scuffle?	what consists of thrusting or pushing
sit, past tense sat	saddle	what is sat upon
	settle	what is sat upon; the name of a kind of seat
A. S. sceotan, to shoot	scuttle?	what shoots out coal
A. S. a-sceac-an, to shake	shackles	what shakes loosely
A. S. sceotan	skittle?	what is shot forward
shove	shovel?	what is shoved, in distinction from a spade, which is worked by the foot and not shoved
shoot	shuttle	what is shot
sour	sorrel	what is sour; the herb rumex, dock-sorrel
sneak, to creep	A. S. snægle, a snail	what creeps
spin	spindle	what spins
spit	spittle	what is spit

swing	swingel	what swings; the name of a weapon which swings on a handle like a flail
steep	a steeple	what is steep
tread	treadle	what is trodden; the foot board of a crank
stop	a stopple	what stops; a stopper of a bottle, etc.
A.S. þolian, to bear	thowls	bearings for the oars of a boat
stand, past tense stood, or A. S. Gestaðelian, to found, establish	staddle	what is stood upon; a wooden frame, *or* a bed of boughs for a rick to stand upon
Dorset, drash, (thresh)	drashle	what threshes; a flail
beat	Dorset, bittle, or beetle	what beats; the name of a large wooden mallet
A. S. rud, redness	ruddle	what reddens; a red earth used for marking sheep

On the form of *hillock*, a small hill, we have *bullock*, a small bull, and Dorset, *huddock*, hooddock, a small hood or covering for a sore finger.

59. The Dorset dialect has its full share of a class of words which seem to be common only in the Teutonic languages; rhyming or alliterative compounds; as *humpty-dumpty*, *fiddle-faddle*.

Harum-scarum. Like hares scared? wild and thoughtless.

Hippity-hoppity. Going on with little and great hops, lame.

Huck-muck. What is in Devonshire called 'Muckson up to the huckson.' Up to the ankles in dirt, dirty.

Hum-drum. Dull; like one who hums, drumming upon objects before him.

Hum-strum, hum-scrum. A kind of rude musical instrument with a long wooden body and four wires strained by pegs over a canister or bladder at one end; and a bridge at the other, and played with a bow.

Riff-raff. Low people, what the French call *la canaille*.

Roly-poly. Rolling over and over.

Slip-slop. Slipping and slopping in dirt.

Snipper-snapper. Little and insignificant. Spoken of a person.

Tisty-tosty. A toss ball made of cowslips.

Willy-nilly. Willing or not willing, from the Anglo-Saxon *wyllan*, to wish, and *nyllan*, not to wish.

60. In a case in which a positive degree with a possessive case is used in Dorsetshire for a superlative degree, its dialect coincides with an idiom in Hindoostanee; as 'Bring the long pick; the *long* oon ov al,' instead of 'the *longest* of all,' like the Hindoostanee '*Yee sub-ka burra hai.*' 'This is the great one of all,' for 'the greatest.'

61. Our dialect is Anglo-Saxon not only in the retention of Anglo-Saxon words which book English has lost, but in the pronunciation of many English ones as well as in its idioms.

A. S.	*Dorset*	*English*
beät	beät	beat
flex	vlex	flax
hæta	het	heat
hrof	ruf	roof
weax	wex	wax

Anglo-Saxon, 'þonne sænde ic eow worde.' Dorset, 'Then I'll zend ye word.'

Anglo-Saxon 'þis temple wæs getimbrod on six and feowertigum wintrum.' Dorset, 'Thiese temple wer a-builded in six an' forty winters.' The lower digits being named before the higher ones.

We retain also some of the Anglo-Saxon genitive or possessive cases where the English substitutes *of* instead of *them*, as in *barn's floor*, *stick's end*.

> he feormað his bernes flore. – Luke iii. 17.

62. From the elisions of harsh consonants, and the frequent use of the syllabic augment *a* in participles of verbs, the Dorset dialect has a mellowness which is sometimes wanting in the national

speech; and this quality, with its purity and simplicity, makes it a good vehicle for the more tender feelings, as well as for the broader humor of rural life. Its elisions and contractions also make some of its expressions shorter than the equivalent ones in English as '*al v̄'m*,' for 'all of them'; a contraction like that of VOM *haus* used by the Germans instead of VON *dem haus*, 'from the house'; and IM *garten*, for *in dem garten*, 'in the garden'.

63. The author thinks his readers will find his poems free of slang and vice as they are written from the associations of an early youth that was passed among rural families of a secluded part of the country, upon whose sound Christian principles, kindness, and harmless cheerfulness, he can still think with delight; and he hopes that if his little work should fall into the hands of a reader of that class in whose language it is written, it would not be likely to damp his love of God, or hurt the tone of his moral sentiment, or the dignity of his self-respect; as his intention is not to shew up the simplicity of rural life as an object of sport, but to utter the happy emotions with which his mind can dwell on the charms of rural nature, and the better feelings and more harmless joys of the small farm house and happy cottage. As he has not written for readers who have had their lots cast in town-occupations of a highly civilized community, and cannot sympathize with the rustic mind, he can hardly hope that they will understand either his poems or his intention; since with the not uncommon notion that every change from the plough towards the desk, and from the desk towards the couch of empty-handed idleness, is an onward step towards happiness and intellectual and moral excellence, they will most likely find it very hard to conceive that wisdom and goodness would be found speaking in a dialect which may seem to them a fit vehicle only for the animal wants and passions of a boor; though the author is not ashamed to say that he can contemplate its pure and simple Saxon features with gratification after reading some of the best compositions of many of the most polished languages, and has heard from the pithy sentences of village patriarchs truths which he has since found expanded, in the weak wordiness of modern composition, into paragraphs.

If his verses should engage the happy mind of the dairymaid with her cow, promote the innocent evening cheerfulness of the family circle on the stone floor, or teach his rustic brethren to draw delight from the rich but frequently overlooked sources of nature within their own sphere of being, his fondest hopes will be realized.

The dialect in which he writes is spoken in its greatest purity in the villages and hamlets of the secluded and beautiful Vale of Blackmore. He needs not observe that in the towns the poor commonly speak a mixed jargon, violating the canons of the pure dialect as well as those of English.

From *Poems of Rural Life in the Dorset Dialect*, 1844.

Appendix B:

Appreciations of Barnes by Coventry Patmore, Tennyson and Gerard Manley Hopkins

Coventry Patmore

Some of our readers may ask, How is it, then, that the world knows so little of this poet? The reply is, first, that his poems are written in a dialect which, while it is almost as different from ordinary English as that of Burns, is spoken by a much smaller section of the British population; so that the number of persons who can take up his books for the first time, and read them off with immediate satisfaction, is not large enough to constitute anything like a public capable of impressing its views upon the larger public beyond it. If Mr Barnes had enjoyed the advantage, for example, of being a Scotchman, our present duty would have been done long ago by others, and *Hwomely Rhymes* would have been household words in every cottage in England. As it is, this remarkable poet has been condemned to many years of obscurity as the penalty of having written in a language to which an ordinary English reader cannot become well accustomed without something like half an hour's reading – a labour to which it is not to be expected that such a reader should submit, in the absence of compulsion from some critical authority.

In the second place, the most essential character of Mr Barnes's poetry, though precisely that which renders his ultimate position, as a poet, most secure, is little calculated to win immediate admiration from any but the perfectly unsophisticated in taste and the perfectly cultivated. The improved condition of taste, in respect of poetry, is a very common belief and boast. It must be remembered, however, that, though time and disuse have made obvious the faults of our predecessors, our own corruptions of taste, if different in kind, may be quite as great in degree; that exploded exorbitancies and conventionalities of language may have been succeeded by other exorbitancies and conventionalities; and that, a hundred years hence, the shortcomings and aberrations of the school of Keats and of that of Pope may be equally striking to the mind of the then easily impartial reader. That, at all events, the popular taste in poetry is not better now than it was a hundred years ago is a fact on which the really cultivated and carefully judging few are probably agreed; and this fact, we repeat, is strongly against the immediate acceptance of a poet of whom it is singularly true that he is of no school but that of nature.

In the third place, Mr Barnes, in his poems, is nothing but a poet. He does not there protest against anything in religion, politics, or the arrangements of society; nor has he the advantage of being able to demand the admiration of the sympathizing public on the score that he is a chimney-sweep, or a rat-catcher, and has never learned to read.

In the often-revived discussion of the relative merits of 'objective' and 'subjective' poetry, both parties have been equally at fault; the half-truth held by each being indispensable to the constitution of the whole truth which they have missed. 'Objective' poetry, in the full sense intended by the one party, and as involving no transcendental or subjective element, is not poetry at all, as anyone with the slightest tincture of poetic feeling must admit. On the other hand, purely 'subjective' poetry is an equally impossible thing, though Wordsworth and Shelley have approached the impossibility, in some of their pieces, almost as nearly as various modern writers in the 'old-ballad' style have approximated to the opposite poetic negation. The divine spirit of love and light is, indeed, the subject of all poetry, rightly so called; but this spirit is not in itself capable of being contemplated by the human mind as a separate entity. It can only be manifested by being directed upon other and external things. 'Light,' says this Spirit, speaking by a plenarily inspired tongue, 'is that which maketh manifest.' Sensible events and objects, then, manifested in their divine relations by the divine light, and expressed in verse, are poetry; and, whenever the poet enables us to see common and otherwise 'commonplace' objects and events with a sense of uncommon reality and life, then we may be sure that this divine light is present.

That 'slight but perpetual novelty', which a great critical authority has declared to be the main characteristic of poetic language, and which is only to be obtained by the perpetual presence, in the poet's heart, of this all-renewing light is, however, also the character of the subjects which the true poet will generally choose; and, if we carefully analyse any very successful lyric or idyll which at first strikes us as being simply a glorification of the 'commonplace', we shall most often discover that it has some 'motif', as the French well express it, which has this double quality of novelty and slightness, although the events and ideas which are set in play by that 'motif' are of the most simple and ordinary kind.

In choice of subject, as well as in that of language, the rule above indicated is obeyed with rare felicity and uniformity by Mr Barnes. All true poets obey it sometimes – that is to say, when the tide of poetical feeling runs high; but most poets, in the greater part of their writings, hide the absence of the feeling which inspires this delicate poetic novelty by 'striking ideas', 'magnificent images', or, at best, by imitations and repetitions of themselves in their few inspired moods. We warn the thorough-going admirers of the modern school that there is absolutely no finery in Mr Barnes's poetry, and that often there is not a single line worth remembering in what is, nevertheless, upon the whole a very memorable poem.

By this time, we trust that many of our readers are satisfied that Mr Barnes is not only one of the few living poets of England, but that, in one respect, he stands out, in a remarkable way, from other living English poets. Between all the other poets there are more or less intimate and visible relationships. They might have written poetry, but not the poetry they have written, had none of their contemporaries or predecessors existed. But, had Mr Barnes been himself the first inventor of the art of writing in verse, he could scarcely have written verses less indebted to any other poet. This is the more strange inasmuch as Mr Barnes is a scholar in many languages, and has, as we have understood, his enthusiastic preferences for particular poets. Seldom before has the precept 'look in thy heart and write' been followed with such integrity and simplicity; and seldom before have rural nature and humanity in its simpler aspects been expressed in verse with fidelity so charming. We breathe the morning air while we are reading. Each little poem is as good for the spirits as a ramble through an unexplored lane in the early spring. The faith we soon acquire in the writer's sincerity is such, that words and sentences, which would pass for nothing in another poet, please us. 'A wise sentence in the mouth of a fool is despised,' but a commonplace in the verses of Mr Barnes is respected, because we are sure that it was penned by him with no commonplace feeling.

Judged by the laws according to which the high-pressure poetry of the present day is, for the most part, written, many of Mr Barnes's *Hwomely Rhymes* would not rank very high; but, if that is good writing which does us good, this poet may compare with the best – and, after all has been said, we know of no better general test of the merit of prose or verse than that.

From 'William Barnes, the Dorsetshire Poet', by Coventry Patmore, *Macmillan's Magazine*, June 1862.

Tennyson

Tennyson and Barnes at once on easy terms, having simple poetic minds and mutual good-will. Talk of 'Ancient Britons, barrows, roads', etc. . . . Dinner: stories of Ghosts and Dreams. To drawing-room as usual, where Tennyson had his port. Barnes no wine. Tennyson said, 'Modern fame is nothing: I'd rather have an acre of land. I shall go down, down! I'm up now. Action and reaction.' . . . Tennyson now took Barnes and me to his top room. 'Darwinism, Man from Ape, would that really make any difference?' 'Time is nothing (said T.): are we not all part of Deity?' 'Pantheism,' hinted Barnes, who was not at ease in this sort of speculation. 'Well,' says Tennyson, 'I think I believe in Pantheism, of a sort.' Barnes to bed, Tennyson and I up ladder to the roof and looked at Orion: then to my room, where more talk. He liked Barnes, he said, 'but he is not accustomed to strong views theologic.'

From 'Reminiscences by William Allingham', *Tennyson: A Memoir*, by his son, vol. I, 1897, pp. 513–14.

Gerard Manley Hopkins

I was almost a great admirer of Barnes's Dorset (not Devon) poems. I agree with Gosse, not with you. A proof of their excellence is that you may translate them and they are nearly as good – I say nearly, because if the dialect plays any lawful part in the effect they ought to lose something in losing that. Now Burns loses prodigiously by translation. I have never however read them since my undergraduate days except the one quoted in Gosse's paper, the beauty of which you must allow. I think the use of dialect a sort of unfair play, giving, as you say, 'a peculiar but shortlived charm', setting off for instance a Scotch or Lancashire joke which in standard English comes to nothing. But its lawful charm and use I take to be this, that it sort of guarantees the spontaneousness of the thought and puts you in the position to appraise it on its merits as coming from nature and not books and education. It heightens one's admiration for a phrase just as in architecture it heightens one's admiration of a design to know that it is old work, not new: in itself the design is the same but taken together with the designer and his merit this circumstance makes a world of difference. Now the use of dialect to a man like Barnes is to tie him down to the things that he or another Dorset man has said or might say, which, though it narrows his field, heightens his effects. His poems used to charm me also by their Westcountry 'instress', a most peculiar product of England, which I associate with airs like 'Weeping Winifred', 'Polly Oliver', or 'Poor Mary Ann', with Herrick and Herbert, with the Worcestershire, Herefordshire, and Welsh landscape, and above all with the smell of oxeyes and applelofts: this instress is helped by particular rhythms and these Barnes employs; as, I remember in 'Linden Ore' [*sic*] and a thing with a refrain like 'Alive in the Spring'.

Hopkins to Robert Bridges, 14 August 1879 (quoted in *A Hopkins Reader*, John Pick, 1953, pp. 133–4).

You are not to think I now begin to admire Barnes: I always did so, but it was long since I had read him (Bridges is quite wrong about him, and off his orthodoxy). I scarcely understand you about reflected light: every true poet, I thought, must be original and originality a condition of poetic genius: so that each poet is like a species in nature (*not* an *individuum genericum* or *specificum*) and can never recur. That nothing shld. be old or borrowed however cannot be, and that I am sure you never meant.

Still I grant in Barnes an unusual independence and originality, due partly to his circumstances. It is his naturalness that strikes me most; he is like an embodiment or incarnation or man muse of the country, of Dorset, of rustic life and humanity. He comes, like Homer and all poets of native epic, provided with epithets, images, and so on which seem to have been tested and digested for a long while in their native air and circumstances and to have a *keeping* which nothing else could give; but in fact they are rather all of his own finding and first throwing off. This seems to me very high praise. It is true they are not far-fetched or exquisite (I mean for instance his mentions of rooks or of brooks) but they are straight from nature and quite fresh. His rhythms are charming and most characteristic: these too smack of the soil. However his employment of the Welsh cynghanedd or chime I do not look on as quite successful. To tell the truth, I think I could do that better, and it is an artificial thing and not much in his line. (I mean like *Paladore* and *Polly dear*, which is in my judgement more of a miss than a hit.) I have set tunes to two of them which appear to me very suitable to the words and as if drawn out of them.

Hopkins to Coventry Patmore, 6 October 1886 (quoted in *A Hopkins Reader*, p. 153).

Appendix C:

Thomas Hardy's Preface to *Select Poems of William Barnes*

This volume of verse includes, to the best of my judgement, the greater part of that which is of the highest value in the poetry of William Barnes. I have been moved to undertake the selection by a thought that has overridden some immediate objections to such an attempt – that I chance to be (I believe) one of the few living persons having a practical acquaintance with letters who knew familiarly the Dorset dialect when it was spoken as Barnes writes it, or, perhaps, who know it as it is spoken now. Since his death, education in the west of England as elsewhere has gone on with its silent and inevitable effacements, reducing the speech of this country to uniformity, and obliterating every year many a fine old local word. The process is always the same: the word is ridiculed by the newly taught; it gets into disgrace; it is heard in holes and corners only; it dies; and, worst of all, it leaves no synonym. In the villages that one recognizes to be the scenes of these pastorals the poet's nouns, adjectives, and idioms daily cease to be understood by the younger generation, the luxury of four demonstrative pronouns, of which he was so proud, vanishes by their compression into the two of common English, and the suffix to verbs which marks continuity of action is almost everywhere shorn away.

To cull from a dead writer's whole achievement in verse portions that shall exhibit him is a task of no small difficulty, and of some temerity. There is involved, first of all, the question of right. A selector may say: These are the pieces that please me best; but he may not be entitled to hold that they are the best in themselves and for everybody. This opens the problem of equating the personality – of adjusting the idiosyncrasy of the chooser to mean pitch. If it can be done in some degree – one may doubt it – there are to be borne in mind the continually changing taste of the times. But, assuming average critical capacity in the compiler, that he represents his own time, and that he finds it no great toil to come to a conclusion on which in his view are the highest levels and the lowest of a poet's execution, the complete field of the work examined almost always contains a large intermediate tract where the accomplishment is of nearly uniform merit throughout, selection from which must be by a process of sampling rather than of gleaning; many a poem, too, of indifferent achievement in its wholeness may contain some line, couplet, or stanza of great excellence; and, contrariwise, a bad or irrelevant verse may mar the good remainder; in each case the choice is puzzled, and the balance struck by a single mind can hardly escape being questioned here and there.

A word may be said on the arrangement of the poems as 'lyrical and elegiac'; 'descriptive and meditative'; 'humorous'; a classification which has been adopted with this author in the present volume for the first time. It is an old story that such divisions may be open to grave objection, in respect, at least, of the verse of the majority of poets, who write in the accepted language. For one thing, many fine poems that have lyric moments are not entirely lyrical; many largely narrative poems are not entirely narrative; many personal reflections or meditations in verse hover across the frontiers of lyricism. To this general opinion I would add that the same lines may be lyrical to one temperament and meditative to another; nay, lyrical and not lyrical to the same reader at different times, according to his mood and circumstance. Gray's *Elegy* may be instanced as a poem that has almost made itself notorious by claiming to be a lyric in particular humours, situations, and weathers, and waiving the claim in others.

One might, to be sure, as a smart impromptu, narrow down the definition of lyric to the safe boundary of poetry that has all its nouns in the vocative case, and so settle the question by the simple touchstone of the grammar-book, adducing the *Benedicite* as a shining example. But this qualification would be disconcerting in its stringency, and cause a fluttering of the leaves of many an accepted anthology.

A story which was told the writer by Mr Barnes himself may be apposite here. When a pupil of his was announced in *The Times* as having come out at the top in the Indian Service examination-list of those days, the schoolmaster was overwhelmed with letters from anxious parents requesting him at any price to make their sons come out at the top also. He replied that he willingly would, but that it took two to do it. It depends, in truth, upon the other person, the reader, whether certain numbers shall be raised to lyric pitch or not; and if he does not bring to the page of these potentially lyric productions a lyrical quality of mind, they must be classed, for him, as non-lyrical.

However, to pass the niceties of this question by. In the exceptional instance of a poet like Barnes who writes in a dialect only, a new condition arises to influence considerations of assortment. Lovers of poetry who are but imperfectly acquainted with his vocabulary and idiom may yet be desirous of learning something of his message; and the most elementary guidance is of help to such students, for they are liable to mistake their author on the very threshold. For some reason or none, many persons suppose that when anything is penned in the tongue of the country-side, the primary intent is burlesque or ridicule, and this especially if the speech be one in which the sibilant has the rough sound, and is expressed by Z. Indeed, scores of thriving story-tellers and dramatists seem to believe that by transmuting the flattest conversation into a dialect that never existed, and making the talkers say 'be' where they would really say 'is', a Falstaffian richness is at once imparted to its qualities.

But to a person to whom a dialect is native its sounds are as consonant with moods of sorrow as with moods of mirth: there is no grotesqueness in it as such. Nor was there to Barnes. To provide an alien reader with a rough clue to the taste of the kernel that may be expected under the shell of the spelling has seemed to be worth while, and to justify a division into heads that may in some cases appear arbitrary.

In respect of the other helps – the glosses and paraphrases given on each page – it may be assumed that they are but a sorry substitute for the full significance the original words bear to those who read them without translation, and know their delicate ability to express the doings, joys and jests, troubles, sorrows, needs and sicknesses of life in the rural world as elsewhere. The Dorset dialect being – or having been – a tongue, and not a corruption, it is the old question over again, that of the translation of poetry; which, to the full, is admittedly impossible. And further; gesture and facial expression figure so largely in the speech of husbandmen as to be speech itself; hence in the mind's eye of those who know it in its original setting each word of theirs is accompanied by the qualifying face-play which no construing can express.

It may appear strange to some, as it did to friends in his lifetime, that a man of insight who had the spirit of poesy in him should have persisted year after year in writing in a fast-perishing language, and on themes which in some not remote time would be familiar to nobody, leaving him pathetically like

> A ghostly cricket, creaking where a house was burned;

– a language with the added disadvantage by comparison with other dead tongues that no master or books would be readily available for the acquisition of its finer meanings. He himself simply said that he could not help it, no doubt feeling his idylls to be an extemporization, or impulse, without prevision or power of appraisement on his own part.

Yet it seems to the present writer that Barnes, despite this, really belonged to the literary school of such poets as Tennyson, Gray, and Collins, rather than to that of the old unpremeditating singers in dialect. Primarily spontaneous, he was academic closely after; and we find him warbling his native wood-notes with a watchful eye on the predetermined score, a far remove from the popular impression of him as the naïf and rude bard who sings only because he must, and who submits the uncouth lines of his page to us without knowing how they come there. Goethe never knew better of his; nor Milton; nor, in their rhymes, Poe; nor, in their whimsical alliterations here and there, Langland and the versifiers of the fourteenth and fifteenth centuries.

In his aim at closeness of phrase to his vision he strained at times the capacities of dialect, and went wilfully outside the dramatization of peasant talk. Such a lover of the art of expression was this penman of a dialect that had no literature, that on some occasions he would allow art to overpower spontaneity and to cripple inspiration; though, be it remembered, he never tampered with the dialect itself. His ingenious internal rhymes, his subtle juxtaposition of kindred lippings and vowel-sounds, show a fastidiousness in word-selection that is surprising in verse which professes to represent the habitual modes of language among the western peasantry. We do not find in the dialect balladists of the seventeenth century, or in Burns (with whom he has sometimes been measured), such careful finish, such verbal dexterities, such searchings for the most cunning syllables, such satisfaction with the best phrase. Had he not begun with dialect, and seen himself recognized as an adept in it before he had quite found himself as a poet, who knows that he might not have brought upon his muse the disaster that has befallen so many earnest versifiers of recent time, have become a slave to the passion for form, and have wasted all his substance in whittling at its shape.

From such, however, he was saved by the conditions of his scene, characters, and vocabulary. It may have been, indeed, that he saw this tendency in himself, and retained the dialect as a corrective to the tendency. Whether or no, by a felicitous instinct he does at times break into sudden irregularities in the midst of his subtle rhythms and measures, as if feeling rebelled against further drill. Then his self-consciousness ends, and his naturalness is saved.

But criticism is so easy, and art so hard: criticism so flimsy, and the life-seer's voice so lasting. When we consider what such appreciativeness as Arnold's could allow his prejudice to say about the highest-soaring among all our lyricists; what strange criticism Shelley himself could indulge in now and then; that the history of criticism is mainly the history of error, which has not even, as many errors have, quaintness enough to make it interesting, we may well doubt the utility of such writing on the sand. What is the use of saying, as has been said of Barnes, that compound epithets like 'the blue-hill'd worold', 'the wide-horn'd cow', 'the grey-topp'd heights of Paladore', are a high-handed enlargement of the ordinary ideas of the field-folk into whose mouths they are put? These things are justified by the art of every age when they can claim to be, as here, singularly precise and beautiful definitions of what is signified; which in these instances, too, apply with double force to the deeply tinged horizon, to the breed of kine, to the aspect of Shaftesbury Hill, characteristic of the Vale within which most of his revelations are enshrined.

Dialect, it may be added, offered another advantage to him as the writer, whatever difficulties it may have for strangers who try to follow it. Even if he often used the dramatic form of peasant speakers as a pretext for the expression of his own mind and experiences – which cannot be doubted – yet he did not always do this, and the assumed character of husbandman or hamleteer enabled him to elude in his verse those dreams and speculations that cannot leave alone the mystery of things – possibly an unworthy mystery and disappointing if solved, though one that has a harrowing fascination for many poets – and helped him to fall back on dramatic truth, by making his personages express the notions of life prevalent in their sphere.

As by the screen of dialect, so by the intense localization aforesaid, much is lost to the outsider who by looking into Barnes's pages only revives general recollections of country life. Yet many passages may shine into that reader's mind through the veil which partly hides them; and it is hoped and believed that, even in a superficial reading, something more of this poet's charm will be gathered from the present selection by persons to whom the Wessex R and Z are uncouth misfortunes, and the dying words those of an unlamented language that need leave behind it no grammar of its secrets and no key to its tomb.

September 1908

Preface to *Select Poems of William Barnes* (Froude, London, 1908).

Notes

These notes serve four functions:

1. They give the dates on which Barnes's poems first appeared in the *Dorset County Chronicle*. This is to establish, in so far as it can be done, a chronology of composition; it has nothing to do with my copy-texts (see Note on the Text and Punctuation, p. x).

2. They indicate where I have emended the few misreadings which I take to be significant of *Poems of Rural Life*, 1879, and of manuscripts in Bernard Jones's *The Poems of William Barnes*.

3. They give the meaning of obscure dialect words. Wherever possible I have quoted Barnes's own definitions.

4. They specify literary or biographical sources.

FROM *POEMS OF RURAL LIFE IN THE DORSET DIALECT*, 1879

First Collection

(Originally *Poems of Rural Life in the Dorset Dialect*, 1844)

SPRING

The Blackbird
Dorset County Chronicle (hereafter cited as *DCC*), 7 April 1842.
13 *drēve*: drive.
19 *frith*: brushwood.
lops: sticks used for kindling.
20 *plēsh*: to lay a hedge by pegging down the cut stems.
28 *drong*: a narrow way.
When the poem was first collected in 1844 the second stanza was printed last. In 1879 it was printed as it appears here.

Vellèn o' the Tree
DCC, 14 June 1840.
1 *girt*: great.
hwome groun': Jones has 'hwome-groun'.
6 *drith*: dryness, thirst.
7 *het*: heat.
8 *squot*: squat (also to flatten at a blow).
snabble: snap up quickly.

Evenèn in the Village
DCC, 7 March 1839.

When he first collected this poem in 1844, Barnes included the following third stanza – then removed it in 1879:

> Tha' da za that tis zom'hat in towns to zee
> Fresh flazen from dây to dây:
> Tha' mid zee em var me, ef the two or dree
> I da love should but smile an' stây.
> Zoo gi'e me the sky,
> An' the âir an' the zun,
> An' a huome in the dell wher the water da run,
> An' there let me live an' die.

Maÿ
DCC, 15 May 1839.
17 *rig*: to climb about.
19 *parrock*: paddock.
39 *gookoo*: cuckoo.

Eclogue: The 'Lotments
DCC, 9 January 1834.
53 *netlèns*: a food of pig's innards tied in knots.

This was the second dialect poem published by Barnes. Over the years he wrote several eclogues, of which six are concerned with the social unrest in Dorset during the 1830s; the other five are: 'Eclogue: The Common a-Took in'; 'Rusticus Emigrans'; 'Rusticus Res Politicas Animadvertens: The New Poor Laws'; 'The Unioners' (later called 'The Times') and 'Eclogue: Two Farms in Woone'. Barnes doffs his hat to Virgil's *Eclogues* in all of them – as he does elsewhere in his work. In Virgil's 'First Eclogue', for instance, Meliboeus grieves about being exiled from his native place, just as Barnes's labourers regret being pushed off their common land in 'Eclogue: The Common a-Took in'. And in his 'Third Eclogue', Virgil describes a singing contest between Damoetas and Menalcas, which Barnes adapts in his poem, 'The Best Man in the Field'.

'The 'Lotments' illustrates the extent to which Barnes – especially at the beginning of his career as a dialect poet – revised his work between its first appearance in the *DCC* and its eventual collection in a book. When first printed, this poem read as follows:

> JOHN
> Zoo you be in yer bit o' ground, I do zee,
> A-workèn, and a-zingèn, lik' a bee.
> How do it answer? what d'ye think about it?
> D'ye think 'tis better wi' it than without it?
> Reckonèn rent, an' zeed to stock it,
> D'ye think that you be any thing in pocket?
>
> RICHARD
> O ees, 'tis a good help to oone, I'm sure o't.
> If I had not a-got it, my poor bwones
> Would now a yached a-crakèn stwones
> Upon the road; I wish I had zome mwore o't.

JOHN
I wish the girt woones had a-got the greäce
To let out land lik' this in ouer pleäce;
But I do fear there'll never be nwone vor us,
An' I can't tell whatever we shall do:
We be nearly a-starvèn, an' we'd goo
To 'merica, if we'd enough to car us.

RICHARD
Why 'twer the squire, you know, a worthy man,
That vu'st brought into ouer pleäce the plan;
'E zid he'd let a vew odd yacres
O' lane to labourèn men.
An', faïth, 'e had enough o' taïkers
Vor that, an' twice as much ageän.
Zoo I took zome here, near my hovel,
To exercise my sparde and shovel;
An' what we dungèn, diggèn up, an' zeedèn,
A-thinnèn, cleänèn, hoe-èn up an' weedèn,
I, an' the biggest o' the childern too,
'Ave always got some useful jobs to do.

JOHN
Ees, wi' a bit o' ground, if woone got any,
Oone's childern can get out and yeärd a penny;
An' then, y workèn, they do learn the faster
The woy to do things when they have a maïster;
Vor woone must know a god deäl about land
Bevore one can become a useful hand,
In garden or a-vield upon a farm.

RICHARD
An' then the work do keep im out o' harm;
Vor volks that don't do nothin we'll be vound
Soon doèn woose than nothin, I'll be bound.
But as vor myself, d'ye zee, wi' thiese here bit
O' land, I can have ev'ry thing a'mwost:
Vor I can fat ducks and turkeys vor the spit,
Or zell a little porker for to rwoast;
I can have beäns, or taties, greens or grass,
Or bit o' wheat, and, sick my happy faite is,
That I can keep a little cow, or ass,
An' a vew pigs to eat the little taties.

JOHN
An' when your pig is fatted pretty well
Wi' taities, or wi' barley an' some bran,
You've got zome joints and vlitches vor to zell,
Or hang in chimney-corner, if you can.

RICHARD
Ees, that's the thing; an' when the pig do die,
We got a lot ov offal vor to fry,
An' inwards vor to bwoil; or put the blood in,
An' maike a meal or two o' good black pudden.

JOHN
I'd keep myzelf from parish, I'd be bound,
If I could get a little patch o' ground.

SUMMER

Uncle an' Aunt
DCC, 4 June 1840.
23, 31, 39 and **47**: Jones has a comma at the end of each penultimate line of the last four stanzas.
27 *blooth*: blossom in the mass.
32 *tutties*: nosegays.
37 *whicker'd*: neighed.
42 *How vast the grass in meäd did grow;*: Jones has added the semi-colon, and I have followed his example.
45 *wer*: Jones has 'were'.
47 *a-vleèn*: Jones has 'a-vlee-en'.
The uncle and aunt are Charles and Ann Rabbetts.

Hay-Meäkèn
DCC, 13 June 1839.
4 *ted*: to throw the hay abroad to dry.
20 *nunch*: a bit of food.
40 *pook*: a stook of hay.

The Clote
DCC, 20 July 1843.
24 *Athirt*: athwart.
25 *more*: mooring rope (i.e. root)

Polly be-èn Upzides wi' Tom
DCC, 15 July 1841.
17 *veag*: rage.
29 *chammer*: bedroom.

Be'mi'ster
DCC, 27 July 1841.
9 and **16** *Jeäne*: Barnes had 'Jean' in 1844 and 1847 – as he also had in the poem 'Jenny's Ribbons'. Jones standardized the name to 'Jeäne', and I have followed his example.
12 *eltrot*: cow parsley.
18 *ho*: care.

FALL

Out a-Nuttèn
DCC, 1 October 1840.
10 *rudge*: ridge.
29 *jump'd*: Jones has 'jumped'.
40 *skipp'd*: Jones has 'skipped'.
leäze (also *leäse*, see 'Meäry Wedded', p. 58, line 36): unmown field, stocked in spring and summer.
43 *slents*: rips in clothes.
44 *libbets*: loose-hanging rags.
Jack-o'-lents: in his own note to 'Eclogue: Rusticus Narrans' (not included here), line 60, Barnes says: '"Jack of Lint" (i.e. a Man of Rags, a Scarecrow, commonly called so in some parts of Dorset.)' In Jones's note to the poem (*The Poems of William Barnes*, Volume 1, p. x) we find:

> For many a hamlet, harvest done meant the time for yearly nut gathering. Landlords threw open their woods and schools shut their doors, and almost everyone would tramp to the woods to gather nuts. Some of the nuts were put by for Christmas, but most of them were sold to dyers. As the latter no longer need them a 'holiday' has been lost.

Meäple Leaves be Yollow
DCC, 28 October 1841.
1 *poun'*: an enclosure for cattle.
7 *eegrass*: aftermath (i.e. the grass left after harvesting). I have corrected the 'ee-grass' of 1879 and Jones's edition to agree with Barnes's later poem of the same name (p. 104).

Shrodon Feäir: The Vu'st Peärt
DCC, 29 September 1842.
18 *stannèns*: fair or market stalls.
38 *snoff*: candle snuffer.
44 *zweal*: scorch.

Shrodon Feäir: The Rest o't
DCC, 6 October 1842.
11 *scram*: awkward, dwarfish.
16 *mid*: might.
30 *lags*: legs.

Eclogue: The Common a-Took in
DCC, 2 January 1834.
11 *What, can't ye put a lwoaf on shelf?*: Jones has a comma after 'What', and I have followed his example.
36 *wicket*: door.
40 *emmet hills*: ant hills.
53 *vuzz*: furze, gorse.

This was the first poem in dialect that Barnes published. It originally appeared in the *DCC* under the title 'Rusticus Dolens; or, Inclosures of Common. A

Dorsetshire Eclogue in the Dorset Dialect, by a Native of the County'. Barnes never abandoned his objection to enclosures; as Jones points out, he was still railing against them in the 1860s, when contributing to a Royal Commission investigating the employment of women and children in agriculture.

WINTER

What Dick an' I Did

DCC, 24 March 1842.
2 *randy*: merry uproar or meeting.
7 *rudge*: apex of the roof.
8 *tun*: chimney.
min: note, you must know, mind.
16 *stoppèn*: Jones has 'stopping'.
25 *clomb*: climbed.
35 *he'th*: hearth.
43 *grindèn-stwone*: Jones has no hyphen.
55 *hidelock*: hide.
56 *na'r*: never.

The Happy Days When I wer Young

DCC, 9 January 1840.
2 *ho*: a weight of care.

In the Stillness o' the Night

DCC, 27 February 1840.
12 *clumper*: a lump.
18 *housen*: houses.

The Carter

DCC, 3 January 1839.
1 and 33 *O, I be a carter, wi' my whip*: Jones omits 'a' in both lines.
11 *limber*: limp.
14 *drug*: a drag for a wheel.
16 *'mether ho*: come hither.
whug: go off to the right.
22 *oves*: eaves.
26 *rout*: a rut.
29 *zull*: plough.

In 1844 the following stanza appeared between lines 12 and 13; it was removed in 1879:

> An' I da zee the wordle too:
> Var zometimes I mid be upon
> A hill, an' in an hour ar zoo,
> Why I be two miles vurder on.

Eclogue: Father Come Hwome
DCC, 5 February 1835.
1 *teäties*: potatoes.
3 *nitch*: fire-log or bundle of firewood. Custom allowed the hedger to take one home at night. Sometimes used of drink, also.
When the poem first appeared in the *DCC* Barnes also gave the following eight notes:
4 *speäker*: Sp-yeker – spiker. At the Author's birth-place labourers hedging were allowed to take home a faggot for fuel every night. It was carried on the back by a stick thrust through it and passed over the shoulder. This is the *spiker*, for which the hedger commonly selects a large and long stick, not only because it has more stuff in it, but also because its weight and leverage balance the load behind.
8 *colepecksèn*: cullpecking. Searching for and beating down with a pole the few apples that may be left on the trees after the crop is taken in. The young urchins turn over every leaf in this apple-hunt. The verb, I think, is properly to *cullpecks*, to cull pecks, to gather in small quantities.
17 *nippy*: hungry.
36 *hoss*: horse. A plank of wood upon which ditchers stand when digging. It has commonly a hole at one end, and a stick in it as a handle, to move it on as the work proceeds.
47 *trees to shroud*: to cut off the lower branches of elms, etc.
50 *by the tut*: by the piece or job, not by the day.
57 *spracker*: livelier.
60 *clacker*: bird-clacker. To frighten away the birds. A flat piece of wood ending in a handle, with another fixed loosely as a leaf on each side. When the instrument is shaken in the hand, the leaves fall on the middle piece and make a loud clacking.
62 *hut*: a birdkeeper's house, made of sticks, turf and grass, or hurdles, for shelter.
66 *out o' the waÿ o' the waggon*: upstairs in bed.

Sundry Pieces

The Hwomestead
DCC, 26 September 1839.
2 *Chalwell hill*: when the poem first appeared in the *DCC* it was prefaced by the following: 'We believe our rustic poet means Belchalwell Hill, commanding a most magnificent view of the Vale of Blackmore, which extends like a richly wooded park as far as the eye can reach. Ed. *DCC*.'
11 *onion-rwopes*: Jones has 'onion ropes'.
12 *to year*: Jones has 'to-year'.
20 *a-feär'd*: Jones has 'afeäred'.

Uncle out o' Debt an' out o' Danger
DCC, 12 March 1840.
8 *litsome*: gay, happy.
10 *quirk'd*: to grunt with breath but without voice.
30 *spur his heaps o' dung or zoot:* to cast it abroad.

31 *sar*: to serve, or give food to cattle.
32 *lew*: sheltered.
33 *dreve a zyve*: use a scythe.
36 *shard*: small gap in a hedge.
52 *bakky*: tobacco.
62 *bleäry to be sar'd*: low to be fed.
63 *scoat*: run away quickly.
75 *herrèn-ribs*: lanky person.
76 *dibs*: coins.

The Wold Waggon
DCC, 2 July 1840.
4 *barken*: cow-yard.
12 *reaves*: ladder-like framework on the sides of a waggon which keeps the load above the wheels.
29 *treäce*: trace.
36 *bavèns*: faggots of brushwood.
38 *Outzide*: Jones has 'Outside'.
43 *a-smackèn*: in 1879 Barnes had 'a-smack'; for rhythmical and grammatical reasons Jones changes this to 'a-smackèn', and I have followed his example.
46 *trenches*: ruts.

Barnes was evidently fascinated by the construction of waggons, and by the specialist terms associated with them. In his *Glossary* (1863) he says:

> To show the Dorset names of the chief parts of a waggon, it may be well to say that its axles are *exes* . . .; the bottom (*bed*) of the waggon consists of planks on strips (*shoots*), reaching from side to side through mortises in timbers (*summers*) lying from end to end over a *bearing pillar* on the hinder axle, and on two pillars (the *hanging pillar* and *carriage pillar*) bearing on the fore-axle. The fore-axle is connected with the hinder one by a *throughpole*, the fore end of which has a free motion on a pin (the *mainpin*), which takes it with the two pillars and fore-axle; and its hinder end, reaching through the hinder axle, is connected by a *tail-bolt* with the *shuttle-exe*, that takes the hinder end of the summers and the tail board. A parallelogram of timbers is fixed on the fore-axle to take the shafts (*draughts* or *sharps*), the hinder end of which is the *sweep*, and the sides of which are the *guides*, and on them are set the slides or felloe-pieces (*hounds* or *bussels*), which bear the pillars when the waggon locks. The sides and *raves* are propped by brackets called *strouters*, or stretchers. The *sharps* (shafts) have in them three pairs of staples, – the *drails* or *steaples*, to draw by, and with a chain from the collar; the *ridge-tie steaples*, to take the ridge-tie passing over the *cart-tree* on the thiller's back, and keeping up the shafts; and the *breechen steaple*, to take the beeching.

The Common a-Took in
DCC, 23 July 1840.
3 *a-bit*: Jones has 'a bit'.
23 *Or clogs, or shoes off hosses' veet*: Jones has added the first comma and the apostrophe, and I have followed his example.

26 *stout*: cowfly or gadfly.
34 *haÿward*: a warden of the fences or of a common, whose duty it was to see that it was not stocked by those who had no rights of common.
35 *drève*: drive (here, to herd all the animals grazing on the common).
As in 'Eclogue: The Common a-Took in' (p. 20 above), Barnes has Bagber Common in mind.

The Väices that be Gone
DCC, 19 August 1841.
31 *drough*: through.

The Music o' the Dead
DCC, 17 March 1842.
9 *lew*: shelter.
In this poem Barnes is remembering his friend Edward Fuller, who had died two years before it was written.

Jeäne
DCC, 15 September 1842.
3 *bist*: are.
Barnes wrote this poem to his wife Julia, whom he had married in 1827, fifteen years previously. (In other words, she was his wife of thrice, not 'twice vive year'.)

The Hwomestead a-Vell into Hand
DCC, 1 December 1842.
4 *gramfer*: grandfather.
14 *rind*: bark.
17 *strips*: narrow fields.
19 *While tother wer a-mow'd,*: Jones has no comma at the end of this line.
25 *ho'd*: cared.
35 *tweild'd*: worked.

Eclogue: The Times
DCC, 6 December 1838.
2 *leaguers*: Political Unionists (see below).
3 *Aye, John, I have, John*: Jones has no comma after 'Aye'.
10 *theäsem*: these.
25 *midden*: might not.
51 *front*: affront.
75 *skenty*: scarce.
77 *jist what 't 'ill yield*: Jones has corrected 1879's ''till', and I have followed his example.
107 *They be a-païd, because they be a-zent*: Jones has no comma after 'a-païd'.
137 *chaw*: chew.
175 *An'*: Jones has 'an'
This poem first appeared in the *DCC* under the title 'The Unioners', and was prefaced with the following note:

> Some memoranda having been put into our hands, being the substance of a communication overheard between two agricultural labourers working together in a barn in this neighbourhood, on the subject of the Political Unions now forming, a friend has obligingly given the following poetical paraphrase, minutely faithful to the dialect of the speakers. And we trust that the plain good sense of John may be as usefully instructive to his fellow labourers as we are sure the dialogue will prove amusing to our readers. Ed. *DCC.*

The original *DCC* text of the poem differed substantially from the one Barnes collected in 1844 (and reissued in 1879), when he added the fable of the crow and the pig (lines 111 to 196). These late additions replaced others written 'with a drift' (Baxter, p. 323), attacking more obviously 'the Chartists, the Socialists of those days' (*ibid*). These included line 22, which originally ran: 'Why Mr. Vincen miade it clear' (Henry Vincent (1813–78) was a printer who published the *Western Vindicator* in Bath and was known as the Demosthenes of the Chartists); line 99, which originally ran: 'Men that do come vrom Bath an' Lunnen'; and two longer passages: the first appeared originally between lines 208 and 209:

JOHN
Var thee dost know the pa'son an' the squier
Do git us coals to miake a bit o' vire,
An' gi'e us many a meaty buone to pick,
An' zend us medicine when we be zick,
An' then ther liadies, bless their lives,
Do come an' gi'e things to our wives.
The squier's wife do often zend us down
A cuoat, or blanket, or a shift or gown.

TOM
Aye let 'em zend ther dry buones to the mill;
We woon't pick buones, we'll zee ef we can't vill
Our bellies wi' fat beef, an' have a pint
O' beer at dinner to wash down the jinte.

JOHN
I wish we mid, Tom; but, ef we do trust
Thiese men to git it, 'twull be zome time vust.
That there's what I do zay, an zoo thee't vine it,
If thee dost wâit till tha be yable
To put thee jintes o' beef upon thy tiable,
I fear thee wooten have noo teeth to grine it:
I think that thee midst larn a lesson
Vrom Mr Piers's book o' Preson.

(Preston is a village near Weymouth in Dorset; Mr Piers was the priest there, and in 1838 published two pamphlets in Dorchester: 'A few Hints respectfully addressed to Landowners and Farmers throughout the Kingdom, more particularly to those in the County of Dorset,' and 'An affectionate warning to the Agricultural Labourers in the parish of Preston-cum-Sutton in the county of Dorset.')

The second deleted passage ran on from the conclusion of the poem as it is now printed:

JOHN

. . . a-sheär'd.
You'll blunder out o' water into mud:
A civil war wo'd be noo benefit
To noobody, an' ef a man can't git
Good bread by zweat, 'e woon't, I think, by blood.
Why I do mind we had a bad meat year
Now thirty zeven years agoo, ar muore,
An' bread, ya know, wer then so dear,
'Twer quite beyand the yarnèns o' the poor:
Var one an' ten wer a gied
Var ev'ry luoaf o' bread a' body zeed:
But yeet we rubb'd along the winter then
An' I do hope we sholl to year agen.

TOM
Well, John, I'm sure I hope we shal;
But ev'ry oone is var hizzelf, mind, John.

JOHN
Zoo be the men that ya da'pend upon;
But God ya know is var us al.

Second Collection
(Originally *Hwomely Rhymes*, 1859)

My Orcha'd in Linden Lea
DCC, 20 November 1856.
22 *hwomeward*: Jones has 'homeward'.

Ellen Brine ov Allenburn
DCC, 14 January 1858.
35 *feärens*: toys. Jones has 'feäirens'.
Barnes told Kilvert (*Diary*, May Eve, 1874): 'the real name' of Ellen Brine was 'Mary Hames, and the poem was true to life'.

The Leädy's Tower
DCC, 3 September 1857.
5 *stickle*: steep.
12 *Should teäke me there to zee the pleäce.*: At the end of this line Jones has a semi-colon, not a full stop.
50 *withwind*: bindweed.
saplèn: sapling.
112 *tacklèn*: cups and saucers.
Laura, Barnes's daughter, noted that this poem 'was written after the death of his beloved wife'. Barnes illustrated the poem with a woodcut in *Hwomely Rhymes*.

Childhood
DCC, 1 April 1858.

Meäry's Smile
DCC, 19 February 1857.

Meäry Wedded
DCC, 1 October 1857.
22 *a-tin'd*: kindled.
36 *leäse* (also *leäze*, see 'Out a-Nuttèn', p. 17, line 40): unmown field, stocked in spring and summer.

The Young that Died in Beauty
DCC, 2 October 1856.
12 *roll'd*: Jones corrects 1879's 'rolled', and I have followed his example.

Minden House
DCC, 11 June 1857.
12 *a-hettèn dree*: striking three.
13 *inside*: Jones has 'inzide'.
42 *By Providence, noo tongue can tell.*: Jones corrects 1879's comma at the end of the line, and I have followed his example.

Our Be'thpleäce
DCC, 6 May 1858.
2 *hatch*: low wicket or half-door.
26 *tiptooe*: Jones has 'tip-tooe'.

Slow to Come, Quick a-Gone
First collected in *Hwomely Rhymes*, then again in 1879.
12 *Did vlee o'er head at night.*: At the end of this line Jones has a semi-colon, not a full stop.

The Wold Wall
DCC, 12 November 1857.
5 *zwath*: swath.

Zun-zet
DCC, 17 September 1857.
21 *droat*: throat.
35 *me'th*: mirth.

The Water Crowvoot
DCC, 21 May 1857.
20 *laïtren*: loitering.

The Leäne
DCC, 23 October 1856.
3 *knap*: hillock.
6 *stunpolls*: blockheads.
14 *As if all that did travel did ride,*: Jones has no comma at the end of this line.

28 *Ov our goslèns do creep vrom the agg,*: At the end of this line Jones corrects 1879's full stop to a comma, and I have followed his example.
37 *sumple*: supple.
58 *reäte*: remonstrate with.

Trees be Company
DCC, 5 February 1857.
4 *The workvo'k in their snow-white sleeves,*: Jones corrects 1879's full stop to a comma, and I have followed his example.
36 *Could come to meet our lwonesome treäce*: Jones has a semi-colon at the end of this line.

False Friends-like
DCC, 10 September 1857.
9 *thick*: friendly.

The Wife a-Lost
DCC, 12 August 1858.
19 *avword*: Jones has 'avvword'.
20 *A-vield upon the ground*: Jones has 'A-yield'.

The Bwoat
From manuscript, *Notebook No. 4*; written after Julia's death in 1852 and first collected in *Hwomely Rhymes*, then again in 1879.
13 *vo'k*: folk.
21 *sock*: short loud sigh.

Pentridge by the River
DCC, 4 December 1856.
20 *drushes*: thrushes.
Like 'Uncle an' Aunt' and 'Uncle out o' Debt and out o' Danger', this poem is a reminiscence of Barnes's childhood with Charles and Ann Rabbetts.

Happiness
DCC, 3 December 1857.
3 *high-peäl'd*: high-fenced.

My Love's Guardian Angel
DCC, 4 November 1858.
18 *in the night*: Jones has a comma at the end of this line.
36 *in the night*: Jones has a question mark at the end of this line.
Jones draws attention to the following poem, which appeared unsigned in the *DCC* in 1848, saying that 'My Love's Guardian Angel' clearly owes much to it.

FROM THE GERMAN

The sun in the skies made his circuit wide
Round the world;
And the little stars said – 'We will move by thy side
Round the world;'

And the sun it was wroth, and said – 'Stay you at home,
I shall burn your small eyes out, if near me you roam,
In my fiery course round the world.'

And the little stars went to the moon on high
In the night,
And said – 'Lovely moon, who dost shine in the sky
In the night,
We will wander with thee; for thy soft ray
Will not dazzle our little eyes away;'
And they journeyed with *her* through the night.

Now, welcome, ye stars, and thou moon so fair,
In the night;
Ye know the hushed heart and the musings there,
In the night;
Come kindle your cresset lamps in the sky,
That I may companion you joyfully
In the quiet scenes of the night.

Third Collection
(Originally *Poems of Rural Life in the Dorset Dialect*, 1862)

Woone Smile Mwore
DCC, 12 December 1861.
3 *thik*: Jones has 'the'.
23 *whiver*: hover, quiver.

The Lark
DCC, 12 February 1862.
6 *orts*: bits of hay put in the fields for cows.
Jones has a semi-colon, not a full stop at the end of this line.

Woak Hill
DCC, 6 March 1862.
Written the year Barnes left Dorchester, where he had lived with Julia until her death, to take up the living of Winterborne Came.
19 *To ho*: to feel a weight of care.

Pickèn o' Scroff
Title mentioned, but poem not transcribed in *Notebook No. 5*; first collected in 1862, then again in 1879.
Scroff bits of wood, windfalls, or bits of pleshing (cut lower branches).
19 *scrags*: crooked tree branches.
29 *taït*: play see-saw.

The Rwose in the Dark
DCC, 22 August 1861.
1 *tide*: time.

The Child an' the Mowers
DCC, 21 November 1861.
11 *sneäd*: scythe stem.
30 *staddle*: footings of a rick.

Laura Barnes commented on this poem: 'True. Happened at Ryall's Farm near Stalbridge. The same thing happened to William Barnes at Pentridge when a child' (quoted in Jones, p. 408). Ryall's was near Bagber Common, Barnes's birthplace, and is mentioned in his dialect poem 'The Water-Spring in the Leäne' and his 'national' English poem 'Ruth a-Riding'.

Leaves a-Vallèn
DCC, 17 April 1862.
26 *An' if we do walk the ground*: Jones has a comma at the end of this line.

Lwonesomeness
DCC, 19 December 1861.
13–14 *avore*/The peänes: outside the window.
19 *main*: sea.
30 *a-while*: Jones has 'a while'.

The Turnstile
DCC, 16 June 1859.
6 *vive*: five.
8 *'Twer hard to keep woone's two eyes dry;* : Jones has a colon at the end of this line.
15 *wheel'd*: turned.

The poem remembers Barnes's son John, who died in 1837.

OTHER POEMS IN THE DORSET DIALECT

The following twelve dialect poems were not published by Barnes during his lifetime, and are (with the exception of 'Jaÿ a-Pass'd') taken from his manuscript books preserved in the Dorset County Museum in Dorchester. 'The Vield Path', 'The Wind at the Door' and 'White on Blue' were published in the *DCC* but not collected. I have indicated where my readings of the texts differ from those which appear in Jones's *The Poems of William Barnes*.

Which Road?
Notebook No. 4.
3 *bennets*: flower-stalks of grass.
10 *wayweary*: Jones has 'waweary'.
14 *An' did toss up their nose, over outspringèn knees*: Jones has no comma after 'nose'.
17 *An' a maïd, wi' her head a-borne on, in a proud*: Jones has no comma after 'on'.

The poem originally had a fourth stanza, which Barnes deleted as he revised the poem:

> An' should I teäke the road to the feast down at Reen,
> Where the pool-foam did spin by the bridge's wide span,

Or where brown woods o' hazzle did hide the brown heäre,
Or the grass wer a-dotted wi' sheep on the down?
No, o' noo such a road did I then teäke the turns,
But where Fanny went in her rwose-bounded durns.

Barnes also published a standard English version of this poem in *Poems of Rural Life* (hereafter cited as *P of RL*), 1868.

Jaÿ a-Pass'd
Macmillan's Magazine, May 1864.
13 *jess'my*: the cuckoo orchid.
31 *heft:* weight.
Barnes also published a standard English version of this poem in *P of RL*, 1868.

Walkèn Hwome at Night
Notebook No. 5.
1 *You then, vor me, meäde up your mind*: Jones has no commas in this line.
28 *weal*: injury.

Aïr an' Light
Notebook No. 5, 18 April 1864 (Barnes's diary has: '*Scrivendo versi.* "Aïr and Light"').
Barnes also published a standard English version of this poem in *P of RL*, 1868.

The Vierzide Chairs
Notebook No. 5, 27 January 1865 (Barnes's diary has: '*Scrivendo versi.* "The two chairs"').

The Stwonen Steps
Notebook No. 7.
10 *church's*: Jones has 'churches'. *speer*: spire.
34 *grammer*: grandmother.
Barnes also published a standard English version of this poem in *P of RL*, 1868.

The Vield Path
DCC, 26 December 1867.
1 *oonce*: Jones has 'once'.
Barnes also published a standard English version of this poem in *P of RL*, 1868.

The Wind at the Door
DCC, 29 August 1867.
5 *I got me sad as evenèntide did pass.*: Jones changes this to 'as the evenentide', realizing the extra syllable is necessary. This makes the line conform to the standard English version of the poem published by Barnes in *P of RL*, 1868.
20 *kern*: grow into fruit.

Melhill Feast
Notebook No. 7.

The sixth verse of the poem was originally written as the last verse.

Barnes also published a standard English version of this poem in *P of RL*, 1868.

White an' Blue
DCC, 14 November 1867. Written 30 October 1867 (Barnes's diary has: '*Scrivendo versi*. "White an' Blue"').

5 *clubmen*: morris dancers.

Barnes also published a standard English version of this poem in *P of RL*, 1868.

The Geäte a-Vallèn to
Dictated to Laura Barnes, 13 October 1885. ('Father dictated to me the poem "The Geate a-Vallèn To"': Baxter, p. 316.)

When Barnes had finished dictating, he turned to his daughter and said: 'Observe that word gate . . . that is how King Alfred would have pronounced it, and how it was called in the *Saxon Chronicle*, which told us of King Edward, who was slain at Corfe's gate . . . Ah! If the court had not been moved to London, then the speech of King Alfred, of which our Dorset is the remnant, would have been the Court language of today.'

A version of the poem was first published in the *DCC* on 14 January 1886, but the spelling given here is the same as appears in Jones (p. 928), which is compatible with Barnes's dialect spelling after 'about 1856'.

POEMS IN NATIONAL ENGLISH

Barnes collected his poems in 'national' English in *Poems Partly of Rural Life in National English*, 1846, and *Poems of Rural Life in Common English*, 1868. In later life he wrote alterations in two copies of the former book – a *red* copy and a *brown* copy. He also set about the 1868 volume, tearing up one copy and interleaving its pages with new poems, then dividing them into four sections and pinning them together between wrappers made of sugar bag paper. The poems I have chosen from these *sugar bag* books adopt Barnes's final revisions.

Rustic Childhood
First published in *Poems Partly of Rural Life in National English* (hereafter cited as *PP of RL*), 1846. Unaffected by *red* or *brown* revisions.

The Eegrass
First published *PP of RL*, 1846. Unaffected by *red* or *brown* revisions.

Moss
First published *PP of RL*, 1846. Unaffected by *red* or *brown* revisions.

To a Garden – On Leaving It
Included in *PP of RL*, 1846. (Unaffected by *red* or *brown* revisions.)

The poem was first published in *DCC*, 19 May 1836, soon after Barnes had left Chantry House in Mere for Dorchester.

Our Hedges
White Vellum Book A.
3 *homeground's*: Jones has 'home-ground's'.
The poem was originally called 'Our Summer Hedges'.

Plorata Veris Lachrymis
From *sugar bag* manuscript. Written after the death of Barnes's wife Julia on 21 June 1852, and printed on a black-edged card for personal distribution. Only one complete manuscript survives – a fair copy written out by Barnes for inclusion in *Poems of Rural Life in Common English* (hereafter cited as *P of RL*), 1868.
15 *The daylengths shrunk from small to small*: *P of RL*, 1868 has 'days' lengths'.
The manuscript of the poem has a cancelled third stanza:

> The waning days that wear so small
> From summer, through the brown-leav'd fall,
> Will lengthen out when time shall bring
> The sunny hours of green-bough'd spring,
> With flow'rs to blow, and birds to sing.
> But oh! my joys no more will grow
> Beyond that blighting day of woe,
> The while my life is waning.

My Dearest Wife
From *sugar bag* manuscript. Written 4 October 1852 (Barnes's diary has: 'Wrting [*sic*] some verses on dearest Julia, "Oh, had she been as many are, etc."').

My Dearest Julia
As above.

The River Stour
From *sugar bag* manuscript. First published *DCC*, 4 July 1872.
2 *Unto me, for thou was nearest*: Jones has 'wast'.
16 *By souls, in joy, without a woe*: Jones has no commas.
18 and 24 the *DCC* ends these lines with a full stop.

The Moor
From *sugar bag* manuscript. First published *DCC*, 23 September 1867.

Lost Shades
From *sugar bag* manuscript. First published *DCC*, 7 December 1871.

Seasons and Times
From *sugar bag* manuscript. First published *DCC*, 20 February 1873.

Index of First Lines and Titles

READ MORE IN PENGUIN

In every corner of the world, on every subject under the sun, Penguin represents quality and variety – the very best in publishing today.

For complete information about books available from Penguin – including Puffins, Penguin Classics and Arkana – and how to order them, write to us at the appropriate address below. Please note that for copyright reasons the selection of books varies from country to country.

In the United Kingdom: Please write to *Dept. JC, Penguin Books Ltd, FREEPOST, West Drayton, Middlesex UB7 OBR*

If you have any difficulty in obtaining a title, please send your order with the correct money, plus ten per cent for postage and packaging, to *PO Box No. 11, West Drayton, Middlesex UB7 OBR*

In the United States: Please write to *Penguin USA Inc., 375 Hudson Street, New York, NY 10014*

In Canada: Please write to *Penguin Books Canada Ltd, 10 Alcorn Avenue, Suite 300, Toronto, Ontario M4V 3B2*

In Australia: Please write to *Penguin Books Australia Ltd, 487 Maroondah Highway, Ringwood, Victoria 3134*

In New Zealand: Please write to *Penguin Books (NZ) Ltd,182–190 Wairau Road, Private Bag, Takapuna, Auckland 9*

In India: Please write to *Penguin Books India Pvt Ltd, 706 Eros Apartments, 56 Nehru Place, New Delhi 110 019*

In the Netherlands: Please write to *Penguin Books Netherlands B.V., Keizersgracht 231 NL–1016 DV Amsterdam*

In Germany: Please write to *Penguin Books Deutschland GmbH, Friedrichstrasse 10–12, W–6000 Frankfurt/Main 1*

In Spain: Please write to *Penguin Books S. A., C. San Bernardo 117–6° E–28015 Madrid*

In Italy: Please write to *Penguin Italia s.r.l., Via Felice Casati 20, I–20124 Milano*

In France: Please write to *Penguin France S. A., 17 rue Lejeune, F–31000 Toulouse*

In Japan: Please write to *Penguin Books Japan, Ishikiribashi Building, 2–5–4, Suido, Tokyo 112*

In Greece: Please write to *Penguin Hellas Ltd, Dimocritou 3, GR–106 71 Athens*

In South Africa: Please write to *Longman Penguin Southern Africa (Pty) Ltd, Private Bag X08, Bertsham 2013*